THE OTHER SIDE *of* YET

THE
OTHER SIDE
of
YET

Finding Light in the Midst of Darkness

MICHELLE D. HORD

ATRIA BOOKS

New York • London • Toronto • Sydney • New Delhi

ATRIA
BOOKS

An Imprint of Simon & Schuster, Inc.
1230 Avenue of the Americas
New York, NY 10020

First Atria Books hardcover edition March 2022

ATRIA BOOKS and colophon are trademarks
of Simon & Schuster, Inc.

For information about special discounts for bulk purchases,
please contact Simon & Schuster Special Sales at 1-866-506-1949
or business@simonandschuster.com.

The Simon & Schuster Speakers Bureau can bring authors
to your live event. For more information or to book an event,
contact the Simon & Schuster Speakers Bureau at 1-866-248-3049
or visit our website at www.simonspeakers.com.

Interior design by Esther Paradelo

Manufactured in the United States of America

1   3   5   7   9   10   8   6   4   2

Library of Congress Cataloging-in-Publication Data

Names: Hord, Michelle D., author.
Title: The other side of yet : finding light in the midst
of darkness / Michelle D. Hord.
Description: First Atria Books hardcover edition. |
New York : Atria Books, 2022.
Identifiers: LCCN 2021044275 | ISBN 9781982173524
(hardback) | ISBN 9781982173531 (trade paperback) |
ISBN 9781982173548 (ebook)
Subjects: LCSH: Self-realization—Religious aspects—
Christianity. | Bereavement—Religious aspects—
Christianity. | Christian women—Conduct of life. |
Hord, Michelle D. | African American women—
Biography. | African American women—Religious life.
Classification: LCC BV4598.2 .H67 2022 |
DDC 248.8/66092—dc23/eng/20211115
LC record available at https://lccn.loc.gov/2021044275

ISBN 978-1-9821-7352-4
ISBN 978-1-9821-7354-8 (ebook)

In loving memory of my mother and my daughter,
Cora Eileen and Gabrielle Eileen.
I will live my life chasing your legacy of love, Mom,
and imagining your unrealized dreams
and possibility, my sweet baby girl.
I hope I make you both proud.

Contents

Contents

THE OTHER SIDE *of* YET

Introduction

January 17, 2020
I am floating in the ocean. It is here I can feel her presence most
often. I feel her in the white sand where her feet once touched
earth; where her fingers once dug for shells or built temporary
monuments out of sand. There is nothing but palm trees and clear
blue skies above me. An attractive stillness. I keep coming back
to this place where we shared so many wonderful memories. It is
magical. The place where our souls can commune once again. It
serves as a dimension in my universe where there is no "before" or
"after." A space in time when the blue of the ocean and the blue of
the sky are only cut through by my still brown body. My eyes are
closed and my heart is full. The warmth of the morning sun shines
upon my face. As I let the water move me at its will, I hear faintly
but insistently over the crashing waves at shore, "Keep going,
Mommy. You can do it. Tell them our story."

It can happen anytime or anywhere. I'll find myself carefully reading
through my old journals or pulling together words for a speaking engagement. I could be sitting with pictures of Gabrielle or silently tracing
the lines of drawings made with her tiny fingers. Her favorite dolly, Barbara, is always watching from the shelf nearby. Pictures of cardinals sur-
round me on the walls. An open window allows me to hear the real birds
outside. Her presence is palpable. The rush of sorrow overwhelms me.

On this particular day, I was rebuilding the Gabrielle's Wings website. I did something I rarely do. Something I will probably not do again. I wanted to find some positive articles or media about the work I'd been doing with the foundation. So I Googled myself. I knew the potential to be triggered would be great. I suppose I hoped that if my search was narrow, the right stuff would show up first. It did not. The headlines pummeled me. Article after article about my daughter's murder and her father's sentencing filled the screen. In the pop-up window, the questions of the public about my private pain were clear.

"How did Gabrielle White die?"
"What happened to Michelle Hord's daughter?"

I don't claim to fully understand Google's algorithms, but these questions were evidence that my name had become synonymous with the worst tragedy of my life. It felt invasive. Even if I wanted to be anonymous, that was clearly not an option. Like the sudden rush of the tide, we all may find ourselves being knocked over by a pain so deep we cannot fathom its end. An unexpected riptide that despite our best efforts for safety and protection is capable of pulling us under.

I realize the duality of my journey. I made a conscious choice to *not* hide. I could've chosen to fade into the background. I could have chosen to try to quiet the noise of what he did. But I didn't and I won't. I will not shrink. I will not whisper. Stories have the power to heal. This story certainly does. My story matters because Gabrielle mattered. It matters because hope matters. Resilience matters. The realization that there is something bigger than us in the universe matters. I couldn't have survived this if I didn't believe that I am tethered to something higher and greater. There is absolutely a God who is holding together the spiritual realm and the earthly one. One who occasionally sends little golden miracles to remind us of who we were before we came to this place and who we will be again once we return home.

Many of us have been blindsided by a loss so great it thrashes our hearts, whether we've lost relationships, careers, potential, or confidence. For me, there are days when it feels like I will never be able to "see" my way through. I'm learning to accept that my life from *before* will never return. I'm embracing the fact that my life *after* is yet to be discovered. And in the meantime, I'm still becoming. And that is truly a gift. If the emotional eons that have transpired between the day I lost her and today are any indication, the depth of my fortitude is still unknown.

This book is my way of standing on the top of life's proverbial hill and wildly screaming in defiant faith that I am still here. I am using the fierceness of Gabrielle's energy and of my heritage to reach deep down inside and find the gems buried beneath my grief. I am a warrior now.

My therapist often says, "Borrow my confidence." I'm also acutely aware that not everyone can or should imagine themselves in my shoes. I know that grief and loss hit us all, and that some people grapple with their own grief by trying to understand what others have gone through. There is a small club of mothers who have endured my particular experience, and I hope with all my heart there is never another member. But whatever has precipitated grief, regardless of who is at the other end of the now-hollow space in your heart, the experience of grief holds similarities for almost all of us. For those of you whose lives have taken this sudden and unexpected turn, I hope my story is a balm. I'm writing to you.

I remember a few months after Gabrielle was murdered, I used a ticket I had purchased beforehand and went to see a Dave Chappelle comedy show featuring Lauryn Hill. I nearly had a panic attack in Radio City Music Hall as I sat with dear friends and thousands of fans. *How dare I try to be normal? How was it possible for people to laugh? To dance? How could these songs that are attached to* before *memories exist now?* My soul wasn't ready to leap. In fact, I felt guilty and ridiculous for trying.

But I did try. And in that trying, I found strength for the next time I'd try. In the initial pivot away from my *before*, I started to accept what felt like fundamental truths for me at the time. I would never be happy again. I would never trust again. I would never be a mother again. I would never feel real love again. I would not and could not heal. Ever. The notion of healing flew in the face of and, in my mind, boldly disrespected my shattered mother's heart.

I was wrong. I held on a bit longer and eventually another more accurate truth emerged.

I will never be the same. I will never stop missing my daughter. I will never see a golden-brown girl with cotton-candy puffs of hair and not feel the ache in my heart and bones. And still somehow, at the same time, I am still me. Changed? Yes. Reimagined? Yes. But still me. And if anything, I learned how to choose joy from my *before* self. That Michelle knew joy intimately. She loved the ocean. She loved hip-hop. She loved children. She loved to cook and entertain. She loved an off-color joke. These were things I got to carry into my *yet*, my new and uncharted world.

So now I laugh and tell bad jokes. Again. I host my annual Super Bowl parties. Again. I cook for people I love. Again. I even make some of Gabrielle's favorite dishes. Again. I allow myself to experience the beauty of a mountainside filled with fall foliage or a snuggle with Axel or the gloriousness of hotel room service. This is the fruit of my holding on.

Although there is loss, we also have so much in our lives to still love. To still share. We must give ourselves permission to once again experience joy. We must forgive ourselves for choosing to live. For choosing to fight. For choosing to have an *after*.

I know it is what my mother, Gabrielle, God, and the universe desperately want for me and I now want it for myself. I see the sunlight on the horizon and can glory in its golden warmth and promise. True, we can only recognize the brightness of light when it's juxtaposed against a backdrop of darkness. Nevertheless, as the famous gospel song testifies, "How I got over, my Lord. My soul looks back and wonders."

Whether it is illness, divorce, children never born, injustices done to us or those we care about, dreams deferred, loves unfulfilled, lives stolen, or health compromised, at some point we all stumble through the darkness, desperately searching for meaning in the pain. More than we would probably care to admit, our faith is too often invested in what we think we control. Our plans. Our connections. Our bank accounts. Our titles or stature in society. Our human equations for what can and will happen. Then, we receive the phone call. The email. The confirmation. The diagnosis. We feel robbed and cheated. Suddenly, the rhythm is off, and the music no longer offers the ease of melodious direction.

The dance is no longer intuitive. The bottom drops out, and we are faced with another set of choices: to live fully in our new normal or to allow our souls to die with our dream.

I do not know what the dance you may have choreographed for yourself looks like. I do not know if everything is going to plan or if everything is going to hell. And yet, there is another dance to learn; a different one, unlike any you may have rehearsed. This book is about what happens when the choreography falls apart, and you need to create a new dance altogether. I know what it means to need a new path even when you don't want one. Even when the one you were on seemed perfect. I am here to testify that even the most broken lives and dreams have the potential to rebuild. To be reimagined. To begin again.

In grammar, *yet* is a conjunction. It is not a natural continuation like *and*; *yet* is a pause before a turn. We can't assume anything about what will come after our *yet*. There's an audaciousness to it. Unlike *but*, there's hope embedded in *yet*. It's saying, "Prepare yourself. Have hope. There's something different on the way." That shift is the very essence of embracing *yet* as an act of faith. My mystic curiosity drives me to explore faith, hope, and dreams and how they intertwine with our lives. Embracing a *yet* season is an act of being present that links all of these. The faith found in *yet* says, "Today *this* is what I understand. *This* is who I understand I am. *This* is what I understand is happening in the world. *This* is what I understand is happening in my relationships." The hope found in *yet* says, "There's the possibility that tomorrow may not be what I think it's going to be." *Yet* is that bridge that doesn't quite connect. As faith and hope carry us away from our *before*, the bridge of *yet* will only take us so far. At the very end, we will have to take everything we have learned and leap into our *after*.

The pivot into *yet* requires us to stand in the mirror and say, "Everything is changed. This is not what I thought I was doing. I didn't expect to get fired when I came to work today. We just closed on the house two weeks ago. And yet I believe that we will get through this." Or "I didn't expect him to say after thirty years of marriage that he wanted to walk away. And yet, there is still love in my life that I can count on." *Yet* demands that we prepare ourselves to walk away from the pity that holds us captive in *before*, and to have the courage to keep walking in faith to whatever *after* may become.

Your *before* may be behind you, and your *after* may be undefined and frightening. But you hold the power and possibility in your *yet*. You can find the grace and grit to defiantly stare back at your *before* and say, "Yet I will persevere. Yet I will climb this mountain. Yet I will find a new path. Yet I will dance again."

This is the current posture of my heart: Despite all of the expected and unexpected emotional land mines I face each day, I will not stop. I will not relent. I will remain. I will endure. I don't always know exactly what will happen. But where I've been has given me the strength to continue the journey.

This book is my testimony to you. It is a love letter of faith and hope. It represents the possibilities that exist beyond our sight line. It is filled with questions that will never be answered and victories of all sizes that silently encouraged me to keep breathing. Because the other side of *yet* may not look like you imagined, but you are still you. If you don't believe me, borrow my confidence. You still can dance a new dance, and despite the stumbles and missteps, you just might find the movement more glorious than you'd imagined. Just be brave enough to extend your hand and heart to the universe.

Let's dance.

Michelle Hord

BEFORE

—1—

Face the Dark

January 1, 2019
Another year, another space in our earthly measure of time.
I'm a year older, but I'm also a day further from my life with
my daughter. I am always aware of her spiritual presence; our
connection. I will never stop missing my little girl. I will never
touch another child who is becoming and not have that painful
muscle memory. There's the realization that the other children will
grow up, and my baby will not. I want to be out in the community,
to meet people. I want to keep stretching outside my comfort zone,
my concept of what's possible. I care less about my professional
work, and more about what I see and hear and share. The impact
I can make on the world. I pray that God will lead me and I will
follow. I will listen and look for the signs of where I am supposed
to go, and how my work and my creativity can move mountains.

I was inspired to pursue journalism because representation was important to me, and I wanted to impact how the images of people who
looked like me were portrayed. My first job out of journalism school
was as a junior producer on the nighttime crime show *America's Most
Wanted* (*AMW*). I walked through the vestiges of murders, the FBI's
most-wanted criminals, and other tragedies. It was a job I was proud to
have. A job that taught me more than I'd ever expected to learn as a jour-

nalist. It was also work that had life-or-death implications. In this first job, my charge was to help connect images frozen in yearbooks and holiday cards with real, live breathing children once again. To help people navigate impossible losses and somehow regain an impossible hope and happy ending. As a young but compassionate television producer, I was thrust into the worst possible nightmares of these families' lives over and over again. The names and photos used for missing child alerts changed, but the fear and impossibility of the crimes remained the same.

It never failed. With voices shaking and bodies shell-shocked with horror and grief, family, neighbors, and friends would all say those four words over and over again.

"This doesn't happen here."

Wherever the "here" was, whatever the "this" was, from natural disasters to evil man-made ones, the shock was always palpable. And I was tasked to sit with it all.

The job was hard, but meaningful. I made $19,000 a year, but that didn't matter to me—I had benefits and a stage on which to learn my craft. I learned the ins and outs of television production. I learned how to get things done. I also learned what it meant to sit with violence. I read police reports and looked at crime scene photos. I endured the crude jokes of law enforcement officials about the perps and the victims. These jokes, I came to understand, were a way to stay sane and keep their food down after seeing crimes that would have been too horrific for TV. I learned how to produce content that touched viewers and illustrated the victorious nature of the human spirit over devastating circumstances.

By the time I was twenty-three, I had been promoted to the role of missing child coordinator and was responsible for all of the missing children stories on the show. I often found myself behind closed doors with families while TV crews were set up outside hoping to get an interview or a statement. Because the host, John Walsh, had started his work after his own son was kidnapped and murdered, victims' families would feel an instant connection with us when we walked in the door. As a result, my role evolved into being part television producer, part advisor/counselor, and part victim/survivor advocate.

No matter the season, my days would look like this:

A child would go missing. I would get paged and find a pay phone (hey, it was the nineties!). After gathering the details from our 1-800 hotline, I'd partner with the cops on next steps. I'd then get a public service announcement on all of the local Fox affiliate stations around the country. We knew that after a child went missing, we usually only had hours—literally—that would determine whether or not they would be found alive. Then I would fly to sit with the victim's family. Over and over again, this was my job. The families were different. The towns were different. The stories were often the same.

My colleagues at *AMW*, as well as the other places I've worked in media, became my tribe. There is a kindred spirit among those of us who rush toward the fire; those of us who want to try to record history. We understood what it meant to have our pagers go off or to have the phone ring and know that, regardless of what we were doing, we had to jump into action. There were always others in the trenches, sweating, crying, trying to stay awake, and making sure that we could do whatever we could to get information out to people.

I loved it. I was an adrenaline junkie, and in a way, I think that's also what made me a fun and effective mommy and class mom. I knew how to juggle it all. I was always trying to figure out where the story was, how to make it understandable and relatable, and always, always looking for those narratives that highlighted the human spirit.

One of the things I'll never forget happened early in my career at *America's Most Wanted*. There were very rarely happy endings, as you can imagine. But in 1992, when I was twenty-two years old, just a year out of school, we did a missing child story on a little girl named Genny May Krohn. Genny was from Milton, Florida, and as soon as we were contacted about her kidnapping, we got a public service announcement on all the Fox stations. In less than a few days, because of all of the national attention around her abduction, her kidnapper started to get scared. He actually told her that she had been on *America's Most Wanted* and bought her a bike at a pawnshop. He then left her at a convenience store near her home.

Getting the call that Genny was alive is still very hard to describe.

I wasn't a mother yet, but it moved me. I remember sitting in the edit room overnight working on the piece. John Walsh flew down to Florida, and he sat down on the grass with little Genny who, with her pageboy haircut and pink T-shirt, seemed oblivious to the miracle she was. She told him that when she got on the bike to leave, her abductor told her that he had a hit man and that if she looked back or told anyone, the hit man would come after her. And she very nonchalantly and sweetly and innocently shrugged her shoulders and said, "If someone says there's a hit man and it's the first time you've been kidnapped, you believe them."

Genny got to come home. There were people who sprang into action, as there always are in these cases. Strangers, in addition to family, friends, and loved ones, were looking for this little girl. America was looking for this little girl, and America found her. Volunteers waited alongside her parents on her neighborhood street for her to come home with the police after she'd given them the information she had on her abductor.

Police sirens wailed down the road as family, friends, and strangers stood with their hands clasped, holding their breath. She got a hug from a detective as she stepped out of the police car holding her own missing child poster, very much as if she was coming home from the carnival with a balloon. Her parents embraced her. I watched those images over and over and over as we cut the tapes in the edit room. There was nothing that gave me joy in that stint of my career like little Genny May Krohn getting to come home and feeling that, in some way, the work I was doing—the overnight shifts, the rushing away from friends to come into work—was all worth it. And those friends have stuck with me all of these years. And like colleagues from other places in my life, when everything went away, they showed up again.

Unfortunately, there weren't very many Hollywood endings for most of those *AMW* stories. I once spent several weeks in Petaluma, California, home of the movie *American Graffiti*. By all accounts, it was the definition of small-town America. I was the first person on the scene for the Polly Klaas abduction. I still see her smiling face today as I remember the hundreds of pictures and videos that flashed across the editing room screens as we put these stories together. The same face that graced the cover of *People* magazine while the entire country watched. I would look at her, looking innocently at a camera, not knowing her smile would one day become a memorial.

There was a candle lit in the Klaas family's front window the entire time she was missing. That candle burned while people raised money, wore ribbons, made pins with her face on them, and combed every inch of terrain possible looking for signs. One evening I went to the house to see the family, and it had happened. The search was over. The candle was out.

The people I met over the course of my years at *AMW* overcame odds that seemed insurmountable. And yet, I learned that somehow people survive. They often did so in very simple ways. They managed to crack a weak joke from time to time. I learned that levity was critical, wherever we could find it. They might hang a Christmas ornament with their baby's picture pasted inside. They got out of bed, combed their hair, and took a shower. People mustered up the energy to stand in front of a television camera, in front of a jury, in front of their families. I was moved and inspired by their bravery. If there is a single, most profound thing I learned during those years it is that the human spirit wants to thrive. Like our physical bodies, it craves strength. It desires to be stretched and moved. We are designed to grow our physical, emotional, and spiritual muscles so that we can carry the superhuman weight that life sometimes gives us.

I was always fascinated by the people who supported these families. The neighbors and friends. The coworkers and church members. No matter how rich or poor, or their ethnic background, a collective village of determination rallied around these people. When "it" happened, they came. And they weren't always close friends and family members. I was always surprised by who showed up. I learned that people want to help one another—that's it. There are people who will cry with you, fight for you, and cook for you—give you whatever you need. Somehow people take the few things not ravaged by a tornado or a hurricane or a fire and speak of gratitude. Somehow people offer encouragement to one another and go out of their way to silently and anonymously do what they can. These people in the stories I covered for *AMW* or later at *The Oprah Winfrey Show* and *Good Morning America* were ordinary people who in extraordinary circumstances had to reach deep for the best of themselves. They had to find their ground and their God. They somehow instinctively knew that if they didn't, they would become unhinged and float away. I watched them as they allowed others to take care of them in every way possible. I watched as they created boundaries. I watched as they embarked on various forms of self-care even if it wasn't natural for them. They somehow went to work, drove cars, asked questions, and took care of children. They fought like hell to survive even when they didn't want to.

Meanwhile, my life was shaping up to look exactly as I had dreamed. Or so I thought. It would take more than twenty years before I'd find myself walking into the familiar sights and sounds of another crime scene. Twenty-plus more years before I too would be thinking, "This doesn't happen here."

HANK AND I always relished telling the story of our romance: how we first met when he served as my brother's resident assistant at the University of Connecticut, the instant attraction we felt whenever we saw each other. Just looking at him sent my stomach into full-out somersaults. He was attractive beyond his looks. Always the life of the party, he was a man with a great sense of humor and manners. My mother once asked if he was from the South because he was so polite. This, despite his strong Bronx accent.

I used to jokingly say that our story was the Black *When Harry Met Sally*. We didn't begin our romantic relationship immediately. He was still in school in Connecticut and I was working in Washington, DC. But we kept in touch over the years as friends, sharing our lives and relationship woes. A decade later, when I moved to New York, we connected and started dating.

There was a security in marrying Hank. Not because he was my soul mate, a concept I'm not sure I ever fully embraced. It was more about having a friend and partner. I'd grown up in a loving home with stories of my parents' friendship and romance. That was my norm. Hank and

I fell in love because of our mutual love for hip-hop and writing and reading great poetry and literature, and our desire to build a family. We were friends who shared with each other our hopes and dreams. That seemed like enough at the time. And because we met in the early days of my career, when I was making close to minimum wage, my career trajectory did not seem as intimidating to him as it did to other men I'd dated.

Hank and I got married September 29, 2007. We were married at the historic Riverside Church in upper Manhattan. It was a fairy tale come to life. Because I handled bridal segments at *Good Morning America*, I had incredible relationships with the most exclusive wedding vendors—including the owners of the now-famous Kleinfeld store. When I was trying on gowns, there was even talk of a reality show. The idea had just been pitched and the concept was still in its infancy. Of course, *Say Yes to the Dress* has become a classic since then.

My wedding day, like most major life events, had a duality. I was excited to begin my new life. The TV producer in me had planned an incredible wedding. I had unbelievable support and love from family and friends. However, my mother wasn't there. She'd passed away thirteen years earlier, and it was still hard to imagine going through that day without her. Her death became a glaring reminder of the loss that undergirded every major decision of my life. Having to tell associates and wedding vendors that she was gone and would not be able to provide any input devastated me on a daily basis.

On the morning of my wedding, I asked my father and brother to have breakfast with me in my hotel room. I wanted my original family minus the fourth leg of our family chair near me. Their love would stabilize me. Calm my racing heart and mind. I'll never forget that perfect crisp, blue September morning. There wasn't a single cloud in the sky. I could not have asked for a better day. Despite the typical wedding jitters, the ceremony was beautiful and was followed by an amazing honeymoon in Italy.

It is complicated and heartbreaking now to look back at those photos. I cannot deny that the day happened. I cannot deny that all of it was real. I cannot deny that the joy on the faces was real. I can't even deny that the love was real. But what I do know is that he is no longer real to me. As part of my own grieving process, friends and loved ones have helped me sift through those photos and carefully cut him out in order to preserve other friends and family in the pictures.

Hank was charming and charismatic like my dad, but the comparison ends there. Hank always had anger issues, but it wasn't until our relationship evolved into a romantic one that I saw the first glimpses of that. I worried about many things in our relationship. I worried about him finding a steady career path—something that was a pervasive struggle for the length of our marriage. It wasn't until years later, during our divorce proceedings, that my physical safety ever crossed my mind. And even then, the one thing I thought I knew for sure was that he would never do anything to hurt our baby. In my mind, it wasn't even in the realm of possibility.

It couldn't happen here.

When I was pregnant, we mutually decided that we would wait until the baby was born to find out its sex. Because we didn't want to refer to the baby as *it*, we called Gabrielle "Baby Bear" before she was born. We would jokingly call each other Mama Bear and Papa Bear during that time as well.

Gabrielle was due on August 3, 2009. Because of my high-risk pregnancy at the age of thirty-nine, I was told the doctors might induce labor a few days early. I used every old wives' tale in the book to try to induce it before they had to. I was literally swimming the day before Gabrielle was born. On August 1, the contractions began. We followed them at home, nervous and excited, and then, in the middle of the night, we headed to the hospital. With no anesthesia, I gave birth to Gabrielle on August 2 at 9:59 p.m. She was eight pounds, two ounces. My miracle baby was here. She was a dream come true.

Like most little girls, Gabrielle loved her dad. Between dancing with him on Saturday mornings, playing video games, and watching our favorite family shows, they had a bond. Planning her birthday was such a thing for us. Hank loved it. Despite the deep fault lines I grew to see in his character as his insecurities began to reveal themselves, the safety and well-being of our daughter was never a concern.

On the outside, our lives were a model of the American dream. Many women ponder if they can have it all—the career, the man, the children. From the outside, I had it. On the inside, though, there were cracks in the foundation of what we were building. Mostly from Hank's inability to stabilize himself in a career path. In 2012, I made a few phone calls and he began working on the Obama reelection campaign. I was so proud of him. I was also relieved that he seemingly had found his place in the sun. When we later found out that we would be able to attend two of the inaugural balls, it was an amazing dream come true. My heart swelled with pride. We took tons of pictures on that cold evening. It was one of those brag moments to post on social media. I kept treasures and souvenirs from the events for Gabrielle. It was historic, and when she was older, I wanted her to know that her parents were part of this great moment.

AS A JOURNALIST, I was always drawn to the stories of resilience. Stories that highlighted the triumph of the human spirit over all sorts of adversity, from school shootings to hurricanes. These stories taught me that even in the darkest moments, there's still beauty in the ashes. This is what I try to remember on a daily basis now.

It's hard to know in this moment just how strong you are, how strong you've been, how strong you will continue to be. It's a little like *The Wizard of Oz* in that "Dorothy, you had it in you all along" kind of way. Hope is there. Strength is there. I remember sharing with my therapist recently how shocked I was that I still had hope. When I sat in the abject darkness, reading through my early journals, I was surprised to see myself trying to find some hope, in spite of where I was. Even if you're seeing nothing but darkness, know there is still light emanating from you that others are capturing. And while it may not be clear to you right now, you'll see it too, someday.

When I sat at the table with Polly Klaas's mom, I understood this at only a superficial level. I still wondered, *How is she talking to me? How is she even dressed? How is she asking me smart questions?* It's only now, at a more visceral level, that I understand. In that moment, it is as if an animated version of yourself appears. The avatar version of you goes out into the world. Propped up by necessity. This is the version of you that talks to police. The one that picks a dress for the funeral. While your heart and your guts stay behind collapsed in a puddle on the floor. But you do it, and the simple act of getting through it is your proof that there is steel in your veins that will keep you going.

Even in the dark, when it feels like you're stumbling, know that you're still moving. Know that there are people who can see your progress. You may not feel it, but you're developing muscles, faith and resiliency muscles. Even if the victory of the day is you took a shower. Or, frankly, the victory of the day is that you didn't take a shower because you really needed to stay in bed under the covers all day. You are demonstrating strength even if it doesn't feel like it.

People will say things to you like "I can't imagine," and they are right. But what I also know for sure is that you will always find what you need to get you where you need to go. God, the universe, nature—whatever works for you—will bring people and experiences in from the most unexpected places. It might be a coworker who has never crossed the threshold of your house but ends up bringing you food every Friday. It might be the neighbor you've only said "hi" or "bye" to over the years who starts to cut your grass every week. The hard truth is that it may not be the people closest to you who become your true strength village. It may be the people who have their own experiences with grief and have a backpack of supplies they can bring you. They are equipped in ways that your bestie may not be. And that's okay. Everyone has a different capacity.

Pay attention to the people who show up for you during this season. Have the humility and vulnerability to ask for what you need. They may not be able to imagine, there may not be words, but there is dinner. There is "Can you make this phone call for me? Can you run interference here?" When something unimaginable happens, people are so grateful to be able to do anything. It's a gift to give them a way to share your load and alleviate your pain. For those of us who spend most of our lives trying to be Superwoman and taking care of others—the ability to not only sit in your pain and discomfort but have the courage to invite other people to sit in it with you is powerful.

There were a lot of moms who had been in my house, ate at my table, and whose children had been a part of my life. But they couldn't all hold this level of pain. Everybody's capacity is different, and I don't hold any animosity against them. Not everyone has the emotional or psychological capacity to hold that level of trauma in someone else's grief. But there were others who showed up, ready to dive in.

Cindy is a mom from Gabrielle's school who I would see in passing every so often. We were class moms together, but we didn't know each other especially well. And yet, she was there for me when everything happened. Sometimes it was a last-minute invite for a drink or happy hour. Other times it was a chat to share her own mothering challenges with me, but first asking if I was "okay" to have these conversations. Sometimes it was running interference or mere comic relief. Gabrielle attended an elementary school called Ward, and we would joke that Cindy was the "Ward Warden" who could help push away any politics or drama so we could focus on honoring my daughter.

People see my armor and are astonished and hope-filled by my resilience. It's only because they don't understand that being armored does not mean you're immune to pain or fear. It doesn't mean you are immune to questioning yourself and this world. Sometimes when the unexpected or unimaginable happens it is hard to reconcile your reality now with your reality before. How could I have been healthy last week and have a fatal diagnosis today? How could my spouse promise to love me forever and now walk out the door? How could I go from being financially healthy to dire straits? No, things are not always black and white. Life is not linear. *Yet* becomes the turning point between past chapters and a future still to be written. It doesn't say "if this was true in your *before* then it will also be true in your *after*." *Yet* says "what once was true remains in that past space, yet something else is true now."

It is normal to have a sense of denial or disbelief at our unexpected life circumstances. Whether, like me, your entire life changes in an instant, or whether you slowly and incredulously watch it morph before your eyes. Give yourself the grace to be angry, to question, to be shocked. But then you must pivot. You must admit what is true and then mourn what once was, before you can even begin to turn your eyes to a new reality. It's critical to eventually be able to say to yourself, *Things are different now. I have to make different choices now. My reality changed and I have a new reality now. I may not like it, and it may not be fair. It may not be what I ever would have wanted or imagined, yet I am here now.* Grappling with the duality of what once was and what *is* will be one of the first steps to slowly moving toward what may be possible in the future.

Perhaps what you are facing has made you question your faith. Or maybe you left an organized religion behind years ago with disappointment and disillusionment. If you once believed in a higher power or a loving universe . . . if you are tethered to beliefs that suggest there is more in the world than what we see . . . it is okay to be angry. It is okay to question your God or your universe. Just know that what you hold deep in your bones and your muscle memory will quietly and patiently wait for you to return.

Every day that hope feels just beyond my reach, grief requires me to keep grasping for new hope. You also must continue to grasp. I believe in having a defiant faith. A faith that refuses to bend or break, despite the ways it is tested. A faith in a God or higher power and a higher purpose. A faith that says even though I don't know what is happening or why it is happening, I know that this "insurance policy" of confidence and emotional fortitude still exists. It has nothing to do with me. It is God. It is His strength and my surrender that let me free-fall and expect safe landings.

Like an aerialist, as I go from one trapeze bar to the next, there is a split second where I'm suspended in air with no safety net below. At that moment, I'm afraid. Yet I continue to reach out for the swinging bar. I somehow know that I will be met at this *yet* intersection with hope.

While I was writing this book, I saw a video from a horrific accident in Lebanon. A fireworks factory exploded and killed at least a hundred people, injuring over three thousand. The mushroom clouds that filled my television screen looked like something out of a nuclear war. This particular news segment featured a woman who was in labor when the explosion happened. You saw her in the delivery room and then suddenly the lights went out. You could hear the explosion and realize that everything had been shaken to the core.

Then, in the dark, cell phones were pulled out. People were putting light where there was darkness. They were literally giving light to birth.

These moments remind me of the best of the human spirit. I was reminded that even in our darkest moments the human spirit will fight for a pregnant moment of possibility. In the end, we are truly all in it together. Wherever one shines a light, the path lights up for all. We share the same goals and fears and desire to be loved. We share the fear of loss. And when we're called to task, we will fight like hell for life wherever it springs up. Hope is like the little sprig of miraculous green that shows up between the cracks in the concrete. That is where faith lives. That is where hope happens.

—2—

Come to Terms

The details of what happened to my family, to my daughter, are horrific. They are horrific to hear. But I think this underlines one of the first points that you must grasp in these moments. When the world turns upside down, when you are knocked literally off your feet by an unexpected catastrophe, whether man-made or an act of God, coming to terms with what happened has to happen quickly. The quicker it happens, the quicker you can start to obtain some balance and make your way back to level ground. At least so you are standing on solid ground. So you can at least figure out what the first steps of survival are going to mean.

It's akin to a house. If you smell smoke and see flames, you're probably not going to spend much time contemplating how it happened, when it happened, or why it happened to your family. You're just going to get the hell out. You're going to acknowledge that there is fire, there is danger, and you have to go. That initial recognition is so important in those life-and-death circumstances, as well as in the emotional life-and-death circumstances. So whatever it is, look yourself in the mirror, speak that truth that you hate to even let part your lips. And then take a deep breath, let the ground steady beneath you, and figure out where you need to start.

• • •

MY HUSBAND AND I married when I was thirty-seven. Though I wanted so badly to be a mom, I'd always been told I'd have a hard time getting pregnant due to endometriosis and ovarian cysts. As it turned out, I had a flawless pregnancy at thirty-nine. Being a mother to Gabrielle was as miraculous and precious as I'd thought it would be. But by the time she was seven years old, I realized my marriage was beyond repair. After numerous attempts at marital counseling, it was clear that Hank liked the idea of being a father and a husband but wasn't willing to put in the work necessary to match reality with rhetoric. It was important for me to model a healthy relationship for our daughter. She deserved to know that she could see a working mom who also had a true partner as a husband and co-parent. My mother-in-law and our various amazing (paid) nannies were my copilots and co-parents on a daily basis—not my husband. I needed to model for Gabrielle what it meant to set boundaries and establish expectations for how a woman should be treated in a relationship. This would enable her to leave a situation that no longer served her well-being if that ever happened in the future. So I asked for a divorce.

After several months of contention that ultimately led to me moving out of our family home, Hank agreed to sign divorce papers on Easter Sunday but then continued to fight and manipulate me for the next six to seven weeks. After months of legal hell, he agreed to sign on June 5, 2017.

That agreement wasn't without a cost to me. It required me to liquidate my 401(k) and offer him literally everything I had, in order to keep the one and only thing that mattered—Gabrielle. She deserved to continue to feel the stability I fought so desperately to give her. I also wanted to make sure he had everything he needed to feel comfortable and secure so that he could provide the same to Gabrielle while she was in his care. So if that meant giving him cash for a deposit on a luxury apartment, or cash for a luxury car lease, so be it. Whatever was necessary.

I remember the moment I walked into my boss's office triumphantly to tell her that Hank was finally willing to sign and that I must leave immediately. I remember searching for a UPS Store with a notary so we could sign quickly. I texted a friend to pick up Gabrielle so that she would not be there when Hank first got home from signing. When we arrived at the UPS Store, I realized I needed to renew my passport and decided to multitask while I waited. When I look at that tiny square of a picture today, I see a woman with a glint of peace in her eyes. A woman who believes she is about to start the next chapter of her life. And she is. Just not a chapter she could have ever imagined writing.

My husband looked worn and defeated as we stood there waiting for the notary. We made light, not-so-funny jokes about how unceremoniously our marriage was being dissolved in front of someone who unemotionally looked at the pages, took my money, and stamped them as notarized. When we walked outside, I looked at Hank's face again. He seemed exhausted and restless. He was unkempt and smelled of smoke. It was sad. He wasn't the man I'd married. Not by any measure. He wasn't the man who'd made me laugh and who could draw me close with just a gaze. That day, his eyes were vacant. He was empty. As we left the building, he apologized for all the horrible things he'd done in the previous months of divorce negotiations. I gratefully and quickly thanked him and promised him that our friendship would remain. Our friendship predated our love and we had been gifted with a beautiful, sweet baby girl we would co-parent and protect together. I told him that she was all that mattered. Gabrielle was seven, almost finished with second grade. He and I agreed to sit down with her the next day to explain how things would change.

We hugged each other and went our separate ways.

I called my family and friends to share the relief of finally being free and then went to my rental home. He went home to murder our daughter.

WHEN I WOKE up on the morning of June 6, 2017, I did what I always did when Gabrielle wasn't there. I sent her a video text to say, "Good morning, Sweet Baby." I'd said these words to her every morning since I found out I was pregnant. I told her that I'd see her later that afternoon. I told her I loved her. In the video frame, I held the other Barbara doll close to my face. I'd bought multiples of the dolls so Gabrielle would never be without her dolly security blanket. Barbara sits beside me even now as I write. She goes with me, riding shotgun in my purse, wherever I go. That doll and Gabrielle's video text are all I have. They are what tangibly remain. They are antiquities illustrating an ancient time and place that are harder to remember and imagine now.

The sweet text response from Gabrielle was comforting. It was a typical text from her expressing love with a series of emojis. She was my emoji princess, sending them whenever she'd get ahold of someone's phone. There was no reason to question this message.

I would find out later that the timeline did not match. My daughter never saw my video. Her father cruelly responded as if he was her.

I will never know exactly what time it happened. I pushed law enforcement as much as I could for information, but there will never be an exact time. I will never know if she was awake or asleep. My prayer is that because he gave her Benadryl, which always made her incredibly drowsy, he did it in the middle of the night while she slept. There was no sign of struggle and I'll always be grateful for that. In the darkest recesses of my soul and heart I think about the hours he remained in the house with her body. The faux attempted suicide. The passport laid out at the edge of his bed. The door left ajar. The premeditated stories of an intruder along with the additional conflicting lies prepared. Him, lying in wait for me to arrive.

When I think about the possibility of me walking into that scene and potentially being hurt or killed myself, I have mixed feelings. Of course, I know I couldn't have stopped him, but perhaps I wouldn't have to be here to bear witness to this horror alone. Maybe I could've gone to the glory where Gabrielle is now and held her for eternity. To look into her bright eyes and smile is the greatest longing of my heart. To hold her again. There are times when I resent surviving. Times when I resent that my desperate fight to keep my baby's memory alive is easily confused for strength and resilience. But I also know that the double traumas, the twin burdens, of losing us both would have devastated everyone who loved us.

I drove to work the morning of June 6. I was grateful that I had to be in Tribeca that day facilitating a workshop. My colleague Helen and I took a taxi from the office to the off-site location. My car was parked in midtown Manhattan. But that day, I couldn't fight the distraction. I was anxiously anticipating leaving and getting to the house. I was looking forward to our show of solidarity to our baby.

At lunch, I grabbed a boxed chicken Caesar salad for a quick and unsatisfying break in my internal turmoil. I always kept my phone close, even taking it to the bathroom. There was never going to be a time when Gabrielle or her caregiver needed me and I wasn't available. I'd only stepped away for a split second, but when I returned I had missed a call from our nanny.

My heart leaped.

I called back.

There was hysteria.

Her screams were piercing.

There is blood everywhere.

"Get out of the house," I told her.

I remember imagining what it was going to take for me to tell Gabrielle that her father had killed himself. And then it hit me. A coldness overtook my body.

Where is she? How do I know she is at school?

I reached out to one of the stay-at-home moms from the school to find out if she'd seen Gabrielle at drop-off.

She had not.

Unexcused absence? With no warning to Mommy?

Sheer panic set in. Then, a core-shaking guilt at my naïveté.

I imagine my face was ashen with fear as I told my colleagues what I knew.

Something was wrong.

Something was very wrong.

I went into one of the small breakout rooms and dropped to my knees in prayer.

Oh God, please. Please, God.

Like the elder mothers and ancestors of the church in their dark and cramped prayer closets, I asked God to give me whatever I needed to face whatever I would face.

It was the longest drive of my life.

There was this literal pain that hit me. A sick, slow-motion movement through this long rush-hour drive in which my colleague, who'd offered to drive me, alternated between speaking in hushed tones on the phone with my boss and trying to convince me that Gabrielle could be okay. "Well, maybe she's just hurt," she said. I said, "No. Gabrielle would call me if she could."

I called my brother to try to find my dad, who I knew was about to get on an airplane for his anniversary. When I finally got in touch with him, he said, "Listen, we don't know what's happened, but I can't imagine Hank would hurt Gabrielle." That is how incredulous this was. A bitter divorce? Yes. Murder? Impossible. Even in that moment it was impossible for him to conceive that a father could *ever* hurt his own daughter. During the usual hectic rush-hour traffic of Manhattan, there were more endless texts. I texted friends to tell them what I feared.

Everything was such a whirlwind as we got closer. Wanda, one of the many dear friends I'd texted, was already there because she lived about twenty minutes from the house. I'd also called Hank's mother and said, "I don't know what's happened, but you've got to get to the house." I put her in an Uber, and then called her nephew, who was the best man in our wedding, and said, "I just put your aunt in an Uber. I don't know what she's walking into. I'm on my way."

As the car entered our neighborhood, the certainty of what I might find was cemented. I knew that by now friends and family were close enough to have arrived at the scene. To call or text me with the news: *Hank killed himself, but Gabrielle is safe. OK. Hiding. Sleeping.*

Not hearing told me everything I needed to know.

I'd been in these scenes before. The police tape and sorrow-filled look from our pastor was familiar. I'd talked to these neighbors and heard things like "this doesn't happen here" and "there are no words." I could write this script—now with personal experience.

When I was a couple of blocks away, Wanda called. The even monotone of her voice said what she couldn't.

"How far away are you?"

There was no good news to be had. The troops on the ground had to be warned, prepared. A mother was about to walk into a murder scene.

But the mother was now me. It was me pulling into my own housing complex with my own family, friends, and pastor. Flashing police lights. Vehicles parked as if they had arrived suddenly. A crowd on the corner. My loved ones, curious onlookers, mothers from school. It was like I could physically feel the weight when we pulled up. The word had already started to seep out. Before I knew, so many others knew. They were standing at a crime scene. They were standing at the intersection of my before and after.

Hank's mother was also standing there, nearly catatonic, murmuring in anguish.

I've given birth to a monster.

I've given birth to a monster.

My pastor pulled me out of the car and held me close. He whispered in my ear.

"Yes, it is true. It is all true, and Hank is in an ambulance headed to the hospital."

There was that same incredulous tone to his words that I'd heard in my father's. I thought I might buckle. I held my feet firm on the ground.

"You mean that motherfucker didn't have the decency to kill himself?" I responded in shock.

I would later learn that my nanny showing up probably saved my life. Unbeknownst to me, Hank had texted her hours earlier to say not to worry about coming over because Gabrielle had stayed home sick. She came over anyway, to get a head start on Gabrielle's laundry. I wish she would have told me he'd texted her. I wish the school would have called me to say she was absent. I wish for many things. But I know now that none of these things would have necessarily meant I would have had a different outcome. I do not know if things would have ended differently. But the reality is, there was no opportunity for me to save her because there was no opportunity to know she needed to be saved.

As the truth became real, I returned to texting people. I began to move with sheer rote muscle memory. *I'm a journalist. Let's get the information out.* I got a ton of different types of responses at first. My friend

Desi texted back, "Oh my God. I'm going to get there as soon as I can. I just need to pull over." I've always imagined her driving and then pulling over on the West Side Highway to compose herself enough to get there.

Flashes of all sorts fly by my mind's eye. Especially as I try to sleep even now through the night. The immediate horror and disbelief seemed to yell through my phone. I remember getting all sorts of responses back. I remember being in too much pain to tell Tara, my best friend. She was Gabrielle's godmother. She was the first person I called when I found out my mother had died.

I insisted my coworker Helen, who drove me home to the murder scene, leave immediately. Someone drove me to the rental house and other people began to arrive. The house slowly filled with family and friends, some associates from church and local affiliations hoping to offer their condolences. I remember being cold as I wrapped myself in the blanket I had made just weeks earlier. A blanket filled with images of Gabrielle and me together. I remember my father walking in and offering me a sedative in a shaky hand. I remember wanting to feel everything and nothing. My father had lost my mother suddenly at forty-seven, and now I had lost—rather, had my baby stolen from me— at the same age. I remember attempting a weak and limp joke of irony about how awful forty-seven was. He was too pained to get it. Carmen, Gabrielle's best friend's mother, arrived. My father said that when he called her, he'd heard a scream unlike anything he had ever heard before. Initially, she was afraid she had lost us both. That night, sedated and in shock, she spooned with me desperately like we were young lovers. Hoping the love and body warmth we shared could somehow create a barrier from the nightmare in front of us. In the middle of that first night, I woke her and other friends up. Asking to go to the hospital. Fearful that I was having a heart attack and aware that it was probably a panic attack. I remember trying to sneak into the ER without seeing the televisions. Afraid to be noticed and to notice myself on the screens that surrounded the waiting room.

I immediately began writing. Sitting with my laptop in the dark. Waking up before the sun each morning to read inspirational or devotional stories or verses. A ritual that felt like breath. Wake up. Cry.

Stumble outside with my journal and my Bible and Gabrielle's beloved doll, Barbara. Cry. Write. Pray. After a couple of days, I gave myself the daily assignment to send one of the devotional readings I had found to my closest friends. More than three years later, I still send those girl-friends a daily devotional.

Later that week, as I walked between my father and my brother into the medical examiner's office to identify my child, my heart quaked with the knowledge that I would never even get to hold her again because of what had been done to her precious little body.

That quaking repurposed to resolve while I picked white funeral dresses for Gabrielle and me. It came again when I tried to gently comb her beautiful soft hair into little puffs in order to cover up the stitching around her head from the autopsy incision. It settled in for the long haul while I wrote my thriving and bright-eyed baby's eulogy. I had lost everything. I had lost it in the most unimaginable way.

And yet, I would stand—even when literally propped up—for my daughter.

—3—

Keep Moving

In the first few weeks after Gabrielle's murder, in my desperation to cope, I turned to the book of Job. I found my reflection and my resolve in those verses.

> Hold your peace, let me alone, that I may speak,
> and let come on me what will.
> Wherefore do I take my flesh in my teeth,
> and put my life in mine hand?
> Though he slay me, yet will I trust in him:
> but I will maintain mine own ways before him.
> He also shall be my salvation.
> —Job 13:13–16a (KJV)

Just like Job, I felt as if the devil had attacked me with the force of everything he had. And learning from Job's sense of purpose, I could only surmise that I was left on earth to do something meaningful.

I grew up with the Sunday school version of Job. The story of his life was always too impossible to fathom and felt like the ultimate ironic, Brothers Grimm fairy tale: a perfect man at the mercy of a bet between God and the devil. This perfect man is so perfect that God lets the devil take everything from him. He suffers in every possible human way. He loses everything except somehow his faith. In the end, God wins the bet. Job is who God thought he was. Job is rewarded and is given back riches and children in "tenfold."

But did he really live happily ever after?

Losing land or a job or a house is one thing. We can have very dear attachments to our possessions. We can work hard for them and depend on components of them for our livelihood and comfort. For many, they define who we are and what we have accomplished. But they are still things. They come. They go. They, in fact, can be replaced. We can get better jobs or bigger houses or even a better employee or spouse. But children? If you lose one child and later have another . . . can you really call it even?

I never comprehended the story. I still don't completely. I don't think I ever will. However, there are components of it that I now understand. Every "Job" challenge looks different. I truly believe our journeys and the lens we use to see them are quite subjective. We sometimes need perspective to differentiate a challenge or opportunity from something oppressive. So the big bad wolf that we fear jumping out and eating us alive looks as different as each one of our life experiences. When I approached the crime scene that was now in my own home, and everything started to slow down as my soul left my body to dive into the deep end of the pool for silent commune with my spirit, I knew I was having my Job moment. I knew it would be his story that would keep me moving.

It wasn't Job's perfection I was pulled toward. That wasn't an aspiration for me. It was his suffering. It was understanding his response to the sudden, violent impossibility of what had happened to him. So as the minutes turned to darker and darker hours that first day, I looked up the verse. I needed a battle cry. I literally felt like my life depended on a mantra to connect what was happening to me with Job's undeniable defiant faith. He didn't mock his God. He mocked the devil's arrogance. He had the nerve to even offer *praise*. I sought out his most famous words:

Though—*Despite the fact that, although*
He—*God Almighty*
Slay me—*kill, destroy, annihilate*

28

Yet—*still, even, in spite of, nevertheless*
Will—*cause or change an act, try, intend, purpose*
I trust Him—*I will rely on the truthfulness or accuracy of God;*
I place my confidence in God; I can depend on the integrity,
strength, ability, surety of God.

As I sat on my knees holding hands with friends on the ground cry-ing, praying, and wailing that first night, I used this phrase as a formal declaration of war. Job allowed himself to wail, to grieve, to shave his head and rent his clothes, and then he offered praise and made his declaration. Yes, I had lost it all, and through the ultimate betrayal to my baby and me, but I'd still had her. I'd had my baby for almost eight years. I had the experience of bringing this beautiful soul into the world and nurturing her throughout her journey. There was still something to be thankful for.

To get further understanding, I looked up all the instances of "yet" and "nevertheless" in the Bible and was floored by how many times God used the worst things to resurrect the amazing things. I didn't look for all the instances of "God willing" or "hopefully one day." I was drawn to the "yet"s because I wanted to understand how in the face of great threat or great tragedy, people, throughout history, had found the courage to still keep going. I wanted to interrogate how the most power-ful proclamation of faith is when someone, perhaps even with a literal burning bush, is able to do the impossible—survive—when they don't necessarily understand why God chose them. Following that example, I knew that it was my choice to exist in spite of that evil.

Consider the wildfires that, for several years, have devoured land up and down the West Coast. So many people have lost wedding photos and homes. Their lifetime of treasured memories and mementos is all gone. It is true that those things aren't ever coming back. It is also true that the survivors still have their lives, and they will be able to build new homes and new memories. Scouring these scriptures was my way of grappling with my own duality: a *before* that was never returning and an *after* that was both inevitable and impossible to imagine.

None of us are promised a free ride. We will all experience tragedies of different scales and magnitudes, with different contexts depending on who we are, where we live, etc. We each have "Job moments." You don't have to be the victim of a violent crime or lose a child; we do not measure our losses against Job's or others'. Our challenge and charge is to feel everything we feel, call in our elders, friends, and families, and share with the world in our own way the depths of our loss and grief. Our journey is also to grab our sword of hope, put on a helmet of faith, and head to the battlefield. As 2 Chronicles 20:15 (NIV) says, "Do not be afraid or discouraged because of this vast army. For the battle is not yours, but God's." In the midst of it all, some things remain and some things are never the same. Our journey to claim the defiance of *yet* is predicated on these facts.

— 4 —

Find Perspective

I do not resent God, although I do not understand Him. I don't pretend to know why this was allowed to happen. Instead of praying for healing, I pray for the fortitude to keep working for Gabrielle and for justice. The ability to withstand the torturous presence of this grief. I believe that God and my beloved child are still with me in spirit. That is my only balm in Gilead. In the moments after, though, I had to create opportunities for me to remember this perspective.

Because I knew how difficult a year it would be, I'd started "gratitude" boxes at both the family home and my rental home in the new year of 2017. I asked Hank and Gabrielle to put something in the box each day. I was starting to grapple with the pain of what was going to be a messy split with someone who was having trouble grasping reality and who didn't want us to break up, and that unfortunately and inevitably, I was going to likely have to move out of the house and live somewhere else while we worked out this nasty divorce. So I started a gratitude box New Year's Day in the family home with Hank and Gabrielle, and each day, regardless of what was going on, we each wrote something to drop in the box. Every morning we would each get up, often with Hank's mom there, and rip off a little scrap of paper and put something in the box. Even when we were running late, we would stop short and make sure we all put something in the box.

When I had to move out of the family house and into a place I shared with Gabrielle part-time, I did a gratitude box there too. I wanted there to be as much continuity as possible. I wanted her to see and feel things when she walked through the doors of that house that felt like home. The first day I moved in, I worked all day to ensure that it would feel homey when she came in from school the first time. Everything was put away in drawers, pictures were up, I had ordered new pictures of just the two of us and of her and her friends. I wanted it to feel at least temporarily like a place of stability because certainly our family home had not felt like that in a long time.

In some strange anticipatory way, I think my spirit knew I was going to need that gratitude box. My spirit knew I was going to need things to remember; to hold. Now I needed to see her little handwriting and remember another time.

So as I opened those boxes while sitting alone in another rental house after her murder, it was a bit like going back in time. It was painful, but also a blessing. Seeing her little seven-year-old scrawl and the sorts of things she was thankful for—clean water and trees and Mommy's food and her doll Barbara—warmed my heart. It was piercing to see the things Hank wrote: the seemingly sane, loving, family- and father-oriented notes of gratitude. But most importantly, it was reassuring to me to know that even when things were unstable and it felt like we were in an earthquake, I was able to somehow wrap my arms tight enough around that little girl that she did not feel the earth trembling. I can see it in her handwriting. I remember hearing from teachers and Girl Scout leaders, because I had been so afraid of how the divorce was impacting her, telling me that she was doing great. In fact, ironically, it seemed like she was blossoming in spite of what was happening. Maybe without having the details, she sensed that this new world would bring something new and different for her and Mommy too. When I opened up those boxes and pushed aside Hank's handwriting and just focused on Gabrielle's, I saw a trend. Her notes of thanksgiving turned house to houses, grass to two yards. In her childlike way, she was saying *yet* with gratitude. She had decided upon her own perspective. She was saying that even though things were changing, she was still okay and there was still something to be thankful for. She had adopted what her mommy had adopted from her grandmother whom she didn't know on this side of the Jordan. This idea that there's always something to be thankful for.

When I look back now and think about those gratitude boxes and my intention of starting them so that Gabrielle could have perspective as we went through a divorce and her family changed, I realize how much it hearkens back to how I was raised and what I was taught. It may feel ridiculous to talk about gratitude in the midst of tragedy and hardship, but it's another way to pop out of that ocean and grasp the oxygen. It's another way, as you attempt to steady the ground you're standing on, that you can begin to survive.

After you realize that your life will never look like it did before, find the little things that allow you to feel gratitude. It can be a sunrise. It can be a dear friend who sits with you and cries silently. It can be a ridiculous romantic comedy that allows you to laugh for a minute, even though you know you will never forget what's happened in your life. Challenge yourself. Work those muscles of thanks and gratitude that will come easier—almost like a reflex—in better times. Focus on what you have versus what you don't have. And even though you might be in the midst of your *before*, keep your eyes on the *yet* to come. The *Yet* I'm alive. *Yet* I have my family. *Yet* I can pay my bills. *Yet* I know love. That's where it begins.

—5—

Survive the Shipwreck

But now I urge you to keep up your courage, because not one of
you will be lost; only the ship will be destroyed. Last night an angel
of the God to whom I belong and whom I serve stood beside me
and said, "Do not be afraid, Paul. . . ." So keep up your courage, men,
for I have faith in God that it will happen just as he told me.
Nevertheless, we must run aground on some island.
—Acts 27:22–26 (NIV)

As a prisoner sailing with other prisoners and his captors, to be handed over to the Roman government, Paul realized that the voyage had become dangerous and tried to warn the crew. He warned them that the voyage was going to be treacherous. The wind did not allow them to stick to their original planned course and a storm was brewing. After a vote, the crew chose to ignore Paul but soon discovered the error of their ways. As the ship faced certain destruction, Paul gave the men instructions that I've held on to in my darkest moments of acceptance. My hope is that you can hold on to them too.

I don't think there is any other biblical story that resonates more with me when it comes to what it means to make the hard pivot from *before* to *yet*. Paul doesn't shy away from the fact that there is danger. Of course there's panic. There are things ahead that perhaps none of us could have ever predicted. Paul told the crew and his fellow prisoners, "keep up your courage." The crew hadn't eaten in days, so he told them to eat. In our context this doesn't mean holing up in your room with a pint of ice cream (although that's not always a bad idea). In the darkest hours, the only way to survive is to go back to literal survival basics to make it through. Try to eat. Try to sleep. Try to move your body. There were many journal entries, especially in my early days after Gabrielle's murder, that began with how many hours I slept or ended with sentences like "I should try to take a walk today." In hard and harsh circumstances, victories are measured on a different scale. So in the moments after a shipwreck, you have to recalibrate. You need to redefine what a successful day or even hour looks like. Be kind to yourself and prepare your mind, body, and spirit for the unknown.

Paul cultivated a reality check for those on the ship with him. Yes, it is happening. It is hitting the fan. Whatever *it* is. This crash is unavoidable. In some instances, perhaps we were warned. Maybe we knew we were sailing into a storm in our lives, or maybe we are shocked and stunned by what has happened. None of that matters now. There isn't time to go back to dissect the steps that led us here or to place blame on the ones who created the path. The thing we were holding on to for dear life, that defined us, that perhaps felt like our entire life, is going to be splintered into a million pieces. There is nothing you can do to stop it. Your only choice is to accept it and save yourself.

Paul holds a "nevertheless" in his spirit, and he shares that with the crew and other prisoners. His "nevertheless" was a buoy for me. As I studied this passage, the connection to Job was clear to me. Job said, "Even though I am destroyed, *yet* I will trust God." Paul said, "I see destruction coming my way. It will destroy the thing that is carrying me through. Nevertheless, I know I will survive."

When we hear about the stages of grief, they usually end with a discussion on acceptance. However, healing is not a linear process. I don't argue that the steps have no value, but I think we sometimes shortchange the process by thinking they will happen step by step in sequential order as if there is some loss agenda or checklist, and once we get to the last box we are "healed."

In my case I can be triggered by one of the million little paper cuts of everyday life and quickly be pulled back into "shock" at what has happened.

But as I read Paul's "nevertheless," I think of it as an early taste of acceptance. It may not be an acceptance with peace that ties everything up in a neat bow. It is sometimes an acceptance on the battlefield; an awareness and resignation that, yes, you are outnumbered and outgunned. It is an acceptance that what you thought you were put on earth to fight for has been captured by the enemy. Nevertheless . . . Yet . . . you are still here, on this earth for a purpose. It may be begrudgingly or against your will at times. It is normal to mourn for the past. Wrapping my brain around a shipwreck that I couldn't prevent and that left me as the lone survivor has been one of the most challenging battles I have faced on this journey. And yet I choose survival over drowning. I choose to navigate a new world with a new set of constellations rather than going down with the ship of my old life.

Hold yourself accountable only to what feels just and right for you. Know that you may rewrite your scenes over and over as you stumble forward awkwardly in your new wares. In time, you will find your footing. You will find your road and you will take with you the pieces of your *before* that you find too precious to leave behind.

December 12, 2017
I'm glad I was able to see Jackie tonight. She's not just a masseuse, but has such a deep, spiritual, and sweet soul. I was exhausted, and it was about a 30-minute trip. However, her gift is so pure and incredibly strong. I want to be able to access it whenever possible.

During our session, she said I looked lighter and that my body wanted to heal. She equated it as a scab over a wound that doesn't reveal how deep the damage is. I visualized Gabrielle and my mom on a beach. Eventually, I felt my grandmother, my mother's mother, pop into the picture. I saw Grandma and my mom sitting under a tree, while Gabrielle and I went to play in the water. I felt tingling in my body.

Jackie said she heard a voice say, "Strength is for the living,"

when I asked for strength for my mom and Gabrielle. She said she
saw my mom and Gabrielle standing in front of me and extending
their hands, and looking back at me to say, "Get up." It's hard to
know exactly what Jackie heard and what it meant. However, I
am convinced that I was seeing these three generations of women.
They wanted me to know that they were there and that they
demanded that I be strong.

There will be benchmarks in your new existence that will affirm what you believe, and who you believe you still are. Look out for those. You will also have people in your life who are unafraid of this space you're in. They are faith-filled people who can walk with you, not because they are superhuman and don't feel the pain, but because their grounding is firm. Perhaps they still have sea salt on their brow from their own shipwrecks. Most of all, there will be numerous times when God will reveal the vastness of His love and care for you, in ways you could never imagine.

IN KINDERGARTEN, GABRIELLE and the rest of the kids in her class put together a time capsule that they would not open for five years. Hank and I were so anxious about this project, wondering what life would be like in June of 2020 when she'd just be finishing elementary school and heading off to middle school. I suspect we thought that she'd be a tall, lanky beauty with eyes just as bright as they were when she was little. Her ideas about life would have grown beyond insightful commentary on her favorite Disney pop songs and the best videos on YouTube Kids. Instead, I opened that time capsule without my sweet girl by my side. Memories have a way of projecting themselves into the present, and the only way to handle that is to sit with them and listen. Inevitably, God will speak.

On the front of the time capsule there's a smiley face with her name. When I opened it, nervous energy pulsing through my body, I saw a bunch of papers. First up, a passage from *All I Really Need to Know I Learned in Kindergarten* by Robert Fulghum, set out as a short poem.

All I really need to know I learned in kindergarten.
All I really need to know about how to live and what to do
And how to be, I learned in kindergarten. Wisdom was not
At the top of the graduate school mountain but there in the
Sand pile at Sunday School.

On another piece of paper, there was a little heart with a string attached and the words: "This is how tall I was on June 15, 2015." My sweet baby, like Mommy, she was tall even at five. Easily as tall as my waist. Such a relief to have a tangible measure. I remember so clearly calling our doctor in fear of forgetting in the early days following her murder. Wanting desperately to ensure that I remembered exactly how much she weighed and exactly how tall she was at her last doctor's appointment.

Then another paper:

A little bit about Gabrielle White, Kindergarten 2015.

Kindergarten event you most enjoyed: the graduation ceremony.

Just like my girl. Ready for bigger and better things.

Your proudest moment in kindergarten: dancing at my
   graduation.
When you grow up, you want to be: a singer.

Of course. I think of the countless videos she recorded on my phone or of the second-grade reality show of a "band" that she and her girl-friends formed during recess.

Mom and Dad's hopes and dreams for you: health, happiness,
   your best effort always, a giving spirit, loving friends, a life full
   of fun.

Always.

Favorite TV show: Liv and Maddie.

That didn't last long.

Favorite movie: Frozen.

Yes! "The cold never bothered me anyway."

Favorite book: Ariel.
Favorite toy: Barbara.

You hear that, Barbara? Not too cool to claim you even as a "big girl."

Favorite hobby: painting.
Facts about me: I'm five. My friends are Jillian and Gabriela.
　My favorite center is the computer center. I'm really good at
　painting, singing, dancing, and baking.
How old will you be in 20 years? 25 and three-quarters.
Who will you marry? I don't know.
How many children? Five.
Where will you live? In a castle in Florida.
Who will you live with? Mommy and Daddy and my five kids.

Five kids in a Floridian castle, huh? You were so funny!

What type of job will you have? A singer.
How much money will you make? $200 an hour.

My girl.

What will you do in your free time? Go in my hot tub.

All of these notes and hearts and favorite things might seem common
to most; typical kindergarten sweetness and hilarity. But it was the act of
opening these up without Gabrielle that made them both cherished and

heartbreaking. The final piece sent me over the edge. It was a letter that was written to her on June 17, 2015, by Hank and me.

> *You're a bright, energetic, and curious child. We are sure that you're continuing as a fifth grader to bring your passionate joy into your classwork, your friendships, and your family. You have many interests right now, art, music, writing stories, singing, dancing, making us laugh. We wonder which of these things you will still enjoy as a fifth grader. We know there will be many new exciting artistic, sport, and other activities you'll explore.*
>
> *Our hopes and dreams for you are simple and consistent. We want you to take care of yourself. Make decisions based on your head and heart and not the voices of peers or the media. Trust the people who love you to support you, help you, and get you through the tough times without judgment.*
>
> *You were the little girl we always dreamed about and prayed for, and we feel so grateful that God has trusted your life and legacy in our hands. No matter who you are or what you are as a graduate from elementary school, you are ours, and we are yours, and we are tremendously proud.*

It was surreal. As I read those words and saw those images, I knew that God was speaking. I could physically feel it in my body. On the one hand, it felt like a waste. Like a robbery. On the other, it pulsated through me as pure love. The kind that transcends time and dimension. There were two realities as I closed the capsule. One where she was five and full of hope for the future. And the other, the one I live in now, the alternate universe where she didn't see eight.

There is a model for understanding how ideas and society change over time, particularly in terms of how they influence politics. It's called the Overton window. It was developed in the mid-nineties by the late Joseph P. Overton, who was a senior vice president at the Mackinac Center for Public Policy. This "window" shifts and expands, either increasing or shrinking the number of ideas politicians can endorse without unduly risking their electoral support. Big and bold ideas like Medicare or the civil rights voting act were inconceivable until they found their time and audience and then became inevitable. When the window moves, suddenly something that seemed impossible shifts and becomes possible.

My entire life and story suddenly became a kind of Overton window. When that happens, the question you ask yourself is: If *that* can be true, what else now fits in the frame? What new things that are beyond my comprehension at this moment may also be true? Could Hank escape from jail? Could he be found not guilty? Could I be in danger from people who may have conspired with him on the outside? These things ranged from improbable to completely unrealistic, but when the impossible happens, that window of possibility shifts.

My life has become one of these shifting windows for the people in my life, especially those who are parents. And as a result, it sometimes feels like my story, my shipwreck, has occurred so outside the bounds of our world that people can barely see me—or reach me—at all. Jonathan Martin, author of *How to Survive a Shipwreck*, helped me so much with this:

> *The first things overboard when your ship wrecked were all the reasons you ever had for sailing. And when the life you knew is a life you know no longer . . . you are right to wonder if there is anything left worth having. . . .*
>
> *While the sails were ripping and the boards splitting, you heard the sound of your spirit dying. The life you had was over. But to your own shame, you were not over, as much as you may have wanted to be. . . .*
>
> *The ship may have gone down, but miracle of miracles, you're still here.*

I remember shaking as I read those lines as part of one of my morning devotionals. A devotional that I sent out that morning. Yes, I am still here. Some days thriving. Some days facing one of the million little paper cuts of pain or despair. I never know when a conversation, a memory, a news story, an innocuous question from a stranger about whether I have children will take my breath away. I have had to make peace with my reality. I will always have moments of shock or horror in the eyes of strangers when they ask an innocent question that leads them into the darkness of my past. But what is equally clear is that this chapter of my story is not my entire story. Just like with Paul, there was a shipwreck that I couldn't avoid. It smashed everything I knew to pieces. But I would survive.

I never imagined that I would be a person who needed to survive a shipwreck like this, and yet here I am. My Overton window has moved, and now I know what it takes to make it through the unimaginable. I'm so incredibly grateful that God is unbothered by that weight. And that sometimes He sends little messages in a time capsule to remind me of the great love He has allowed me to experience in this lifetime. Yes, there are a million little paper cuts in there. But there are also a million little joys. A million little ways God has shown up in my life. A million little reminders that I have known love and could perhaps one day know it again. There is pain there. A wound that feels like it will never heal. But there is a truth beyond what I can see also. A reality that lives beyond what I can process in this or any other moment. That I'm never alone. That God is always there.

I'm writing this book in the middle of a global pandemic. Most of us could never have imagined surviving something of that magnitude—the isolation, the scarcity, the misinformation, the fear. And yet here you are—the window of what you can imagine surviving has moved.

Sometimes, despite your best efforts, there will be a shipwreck.

Things that you thought you knew for sure may be lost or destroyed.

Hardship does not discriminate.

Nevertheless, I challenge you to look in the mirror past perhaps the physical manifestations of pain or sorrow or loss. Look yourself in the eyes and say with a defiant faith, "The ship is no more. But I am still here. I don't know what the future holds, but I am willing to face it head-on. Eyes front, heart open to what the universe brings my way. While the broken vessel will lie in shambles at the edge of the shore, I will not. I will keep going. I will remain."

— 6 —

Lose the Playbook
(Everything Is Different)

As you try to define yourself amid the wreckage of your life, the world takes everything from the news to neighborhood gossip and attempts to define you and what has happened to you for themselves. Suddenly, your pain becomes a public matter. It feels like you have an infectious disease. People wonder how you "got it." How long perhaps you or your situation were "asymptomatic." And there is the real but unsaid fear that if someone like you was susceptible to catching what I call the "tragedy disease," they could catch it too. It's an illness that people fear in the way that people fear catching any virus. They see it on television. They whisper about the person who has it at the coffee shop. They wake up in a cold sweat after a nightmare, relieved that, for them, it isn't real. When my mother died, I was devastated that some of the people I had anticipated would be there for me the most were not able to. Not because they didn't love me or didn't want to be there, but because they literally did not have the emotional or spiritual capacity to sit in my pain with me. They couldn't hold the weight of my grief. Whether they were haunted by the memory of their own stories brought to light by my loss, or fearful that my truth could become theirs, in an act of self-preservation, they chose to disconnect from me. At times it really did feel like people thought perhaps they could catch it. Her mom died unexpectedly and healthy at fifty? *Maybe mine will too.* Her husband killed her daughter? *Those things don't happen to people I know. . . . She must not be who I thought she was.* Many of those in proximity—those who stayed close and those who eventually didn't—wondered in the quiet recesses of their minds if the tragedy disease could somehow catch them too.

As I began to reemerge over that first year, I could see the shift happening almost in real time. Brave attempts to stand purse-lipped and stoic as we broke ground on the playground. Standing in the background while their own daughters and sons who had spent time with Gabrielle and perhaps even attended a party or playdate at my house ran toward me. They lurked back. They called and emailed less.

Sometimes life pushes you slowly or transports you violently all at once from what you once knew into the unknown. All of the sudden, it feels like you are on stage in a play you've rehearsed a million times. With characters and choreography you know well, but now you are in a different costume. Now you are a foreign character who is both familiar and frightening to the rest of the cast.

Give yourself grace. Over time, you will decide what pieces of this story and choreography are more painful to take with you, despite their familiarity, than to leave behind as you move toward a new setting. It will happen, but it won't happen all at once. You may, in fact, find that something is comforting one day and haunting the next. As my therapist told me often early on, "There is no playbook."

— 7 —

Choose Hope

Gabrielle Eileen, my Gabi Bear, has been my heart's hope chest. Her life is a testimony where I have carefully smoothed out the rough edges when possible, where I have tried to blaze a path of pride and create new rituals, where I tried to connect her to her elders who walked the earth like giants before us. I often shared with her, "We are tough girls. We come from a long line of women who trust God and who know how to make it through."

Between the lessons, the lectures, the classes, the trips, the organizations, the awards, the programs, were the silent moments. The times when, young woman to older woman, we considered our lot. When we silently pondered what it meant to be female and Black and strong. What it meant to have sandy curly hair and a fiery spirit. Within these almost eight years, I have had the privilege to carefully prepare and pack all of my hope, all of my best intentions, all of my dreams, all of my fears, and all of my future.

Now I imagine Gabrielle Eileen and Cora Eileen sitting together and opening the hope chest, marveling at what their mother and daughter did for them both in honor and profound grief. They are together now. Free. Safe. At rest.

Yet, I remain. I shall not waver in my faith. I shall not waver in my path. I shall not waver. Because that's what my mother and her mother and her mother's mother put deep in the soul of my hope chest. Though he slay me, yet will I trust him.

—From the eulogy of Gabrielle Eileen White, June 2017

One of the scriptures I've often wrestled with in the Bible is in 1 Corinthians 13—the famous love passage. It says, "And now these three remain: faith, hope and love. But the greatest of these is love." (1 Cor 13:13) Love is powerful, yes. And the agape love of God certainly supersedes anything else. But for me, hope is the most enduring. Hope is the stabilizer. It literally keeps us breathing when everything around us is trying to steal our breath. Broken and evil people can manipulate love. They can murder love. They can twist the word and use it as a threat or a weapon. Love, as I've known it, is like water. It's only held safely when it's in a vessel that's not cracked or broken.

As a tall, lanky, awkward, and nerdy teenager who could spend hours reading Hallmark cards in the store, I often hoped for love. I experienced tremendous familial love from my parents, brother, grandparents, and extended family. I had dear friends I loved and who loved me back. However, the romantic love that is the stuff of every teenage girl's fantasies, the kind we found on the big screen or, for me, on *The Young and the Restless* while supposedly doing homework, was the thing I was always looking for. What I learned over time through the normal heartaches of romantic relationships was that love is subjective. Love is fluid, defined differently by each person. Love can mean obligation. Love can mean responsibility. Love can mean fidelity. Love can mean cherishing. But, depending on your background, family of origin, and life experiences, love can also be defined in much darker terms. It can mean possession. It can mean pain. For some, love has only been expressed through verbal or physical abuse. Any attention at all—even negative—for some is a sign of love. Every naïve girl or woman who's slipped her hand into the hand of someone a little slicker with some nefarious intentions has heard "I love you" uttered as easily as some folks say, "What's for dinner?"

Also, in the context of loss or grief, we may or may not have faith in a higher power. I certainly believe having faith in something bigger than ourselves is a great tethering device and also helps give us perspective. However, hope is something more audacious. Hope says I am going to paint a picture of a future that is not here yet. My faith says there is a higher power steering me; my hope says I can paint a picture of something I've never seen. You can live without love, but it's hard to live without hope. You can hope for love. Hope allows people to even perhaps stay in relationships after the love is gone because hope says maybe things can change. Maybe things can turn around. Hope is what gives people the courage to move beyond loss or addiction or depression. Love certainly supports it, and as someone who feels overwhelmed by the amount of love from so many people in my life, I would never discount love. However, in emotional and spiritual war, we may love the thing we're fighting for, but that love alone won't get us to the other side of the hill. Hope will. In these kinds of battles, we must be hope warriors.

On a trip to the Bahamas, I had the opportunity to see work by a local artist named Angelika Wallace-Whitfield. Her art started as a graffiti campaign before the devastating and fatal Hurricane Dorian struck the islands in 2019. The title of her collection was even more powerful in the wake of the storm and resonated with me so much: *Hope Is a Weapon*.

That is the type of hope I have to lean in to every day. It's the hope that allowed me to testify in a criminal trial and read in front of news cameras a victim impact statement about the devastation of losing my precious Gabrielle. It's the hope that allows me to search through the ashes for traces of light and love, even though my life was cruelly burned to the ground. The hope that allows me to see Gabrielle's bright eyes and infectious smile in girls and boys around the world through my foundation, Gabrielle's Wings. It's most certainly a powerful hope. A dangerous hope. An audacious hope. It's extremely important to me on this grief journey to use this hope to weaponize children in need all over the globe. I want this hope, in Gabrielle's name, to empower them to dream bigger dreams and to scale higher summits. If we can reach deep down past the pain, we may not find love, but we can find that warrior hope.

One of my favorite movies, *Forrest Gump*, has the now-famous line: "Life is like a box of chocolates. You never know what you're gonna get." That resonates with me now more than ever. We wake up each morning with a plan for the day. An agenda perhaps for work, family, and ourselves. Some days everything goes exactly as planned. Other days, there are pleasant and unexpected surprises or unpleasant distractions. Occasionally, a day comes that is unimaginable. A day that shakes you to your core.

When I was an executive at NBCUniversal, I had a large team spread throughout the country. I would often travel to our studio lot in LA, where I had a dozen or so team members. One particular trip would allow me to share some good news. I was going to promote one of my superstar team members into a bigger role. I had back-to-back meetings that day and was running late. When I realized I wouldn't be on time for my meeting with Jennifer, the team member who was being promoted, I sent a quick text to her assistant asking her to let her boss know I was running behind schedule. Miraculously, that text may have been lifesaving. Everything slowed down when I saw the terrified face of another woman on my team as she ran to my office. I could feel the panic before she even opened her mouth.

"Something's happened. Jennifer needs you."

We ran back over to the team's workspace. There were people crying. Others talking frantically. But straight ahead was Jennifer's office. There were people gathered around her as she lay on the floor convulsing. Various team members were running in and out, trying to talk through how to manage the situation with a 911 operator on speakerphone while we waited for an ambulance. Because of the positioning of Jennifer's office, had I not asked her assistant to pop in with my message, it's possible we could have found her too late.

Life always slows down for me in these moments. It's as if my mind detaches and I can take a step back and watch what is happening, as if I'm not there. In that separate compartmentalized space, I'm able to think clearly. Taking that step back, out of the space, allows me room to breathe and think. It feels like jumping into the deep end of a swimming pool. Sounds are muted. The lens through which I see is different. The most prevalent sound is my own breath and my own beating heart. I was steeling myself for action but also remembering that Jennifer was a wife and mother, and that my own mother had died of a brain aneurysm. I wondered what her last minutes were like. But when

I am in a moment of crisis, I can separate my feelings of terror from the need to act quickly.

As I worked with my coworkers to try to stabilize my colleague, in my separate space I was saying to myself, *You have to be prepared for anything. God, please save her. Lord, regardless of what may happen, help me to remain intact and strong. Help me to rise to the occasion.* I couldn't see what would come next, but I had hope—a fierce, powerful hope—that we'd all reacted quickly enough. When the ambulance finally arrived, I made it clear that I was going with them to take Jennifer to the hospital. I knew from my news coverage days that one person was allowed to ride with a patient in the back of the ambulance in most circumstances. If the worst was going to happen, I wanted Jennifer to be with someone she knew.

In the ambulance, I looked down at Jennifer's terrified face and kept talking to her. I let her know that I was there with her. I don't know what she could hear or understand in that moment, but I hoped with all of my heart that it would give her some type of peace. I hoped that if the worst was coming, I would hold her hand and meet her gaze until it was done.

We arrived at the hospital and went through the ER dance. Yes, I could wait in one area, but no, I couldn't come into the exam room. I wasn't given much information initially because we weren't related. As I badgered a doctor to give me something to share with Jennifer's husband, who was on his way, the doctor had to rush back into the room as she started seizing again. The door shut in my face and I could only hear the sounds of urgency.

I had never met her husband before, and when he arrived, he was obviously and understandably in shock. I was Jennifer's boss and a "work friend," and I know he must have had mixed feelings about sharing such an intimate space with a stranger. As we sat together in a closed-off waiting room, it seemed like time ticked away excruciatingly slowly. We waited for word from the doctor. John had not even been able to see Jennifer yet.

Suddenly, the door burst open and a scruffy, youngish man with glasses came into the room. He announced that he was the chaplain for the hospital. I held my breath, fearing the worst, as he began to speak to us. When his second statement after his name and title was that Jennifer was still being tested and he wanted us to know about the chaplain services, I momentarily forgot that this was a man of God. With a series of words one can't find in the Bible, I gave him some constructive feedback that suggested the first words to a husband who hasn't seen his wife yet after a traumatic neurological event should not be that he was the freaking chaplain. After I offered my little career advice to the dear young chaplain, he left. Staring into the distance after the door shut behind the rattled, chastised chaplain, Jennifer's husband said, "Yeah, I want you to stay."

Over the next several days I had to manage my team's trauma and needs. I did my best to support Jennifer's husband, and even snuck an In-N-Out burger into the ICU for him. We gratefully were able to joke about my beef contraband later, as he would ask me if my bag still smelled like those damn cheeseburgers. Thankfully, with a great deal of time and therapy, Jennifer made a complete recovery. However, after several sleepless nights, I remember getting on my flight home from LA to NY. All I wanted to do was get home to my family. To hug my little girl, who was about six years old at the time.

I took a 6 a.m. flight back to ensure I could get to her before bedtime. As the plane took off, the sun was breaking through the night. I began to cry uncontrollably. I am sure the passenger next to me wondered what was wrong, but it felt like the first time I could exhale. I had held on to my faith and strength as much as possible and steeled myself in front of my team and Jennifer's family while I was in LA. However, in this quiet space I suddenly began to thaw and feel my own trauma from the experience. It's as if I'd popped up from that deep end of the pool and felt the cold air hit and shock my face again. As I watched the orange-and-yellow brilliance break through to create patterns of promise in the sky, I hoped that there would be a day when we could laugh about the funny parts of what we had just gone through, and shudder with gratefulness about the rest. I hoped that I would be able to regain my composure when I got back to the office in New York. We had made it through, and now it was time to begin healing.

It's so hard to see in the dark. Whether that dark is an unexpected accident or event, bad news, or a scary diagnosis, it is so hard to imagine dawn still existing at all. However, to me, this is where the power of hope reigns. Yes, faith says, "It is well with my soul." Faith says, "Regardless of what happened there will be new chapters and new pages to turn." But hope imagines the horizon that is not yet seen. Hope fashions possibility. Images that are possible, but not probable. As I wiped my face and felt the warmth of the rising sun, I came back to my core. It had been a terrifying week. One I could have never imagined. I had been thrust into the front row of a devastating and life-threatening situation involving someone I cared about a great deal. I had to manage it for executives and colleagues and tried my best to be sensitive and caring to her family. But when I looked up and out that window, I was met with hope. I was reminded that there was something more powerful than me guiding the journey. I was reminded that there is always a new dawn and that, yes, answers may still be just beyond the horizon, but I was moving to meet them. I loved my friend Jennifer. I loved my team. But my love couldn't propel me to dive into action. My love didn't allow me to imagine her well or imagine myself handling the situation with poise. My hope did that. My hope for a brighter day did that, and my hope for the best version of myself.

For someone who grew up in the church as the granddaughter of a Baptist minister, to buck one of the most well-known verses of the Bible is controversial at best. However, for me, hope is the center of everything. When you look up faith and hope in the dictionary, you find that faith is confidence or trust in a person or thing, or a belief not based on proof. One of my favorite verses in the Bible is Hebrews 11:1: "Now faith is the substance of things hoped for, the evidence of things not seen." That somewhat sums up the battle. Hope is that optimistic attitude or that state of mind that's based on an expectation or desire. So faith says, it is so *now*, and hope says it *could* happen in the future. It's the latter belief that often feels more attainable when the pain of loss is so great.

Yes, I did everything within my power and the confines of the law to try to protect Gabrielle and myself. I will always be haunted with the questions of what I could have done differently; what I may have missed. Regardless of the circumstances, the long hall of regret is one of the haunted spaces we all must pass through on our grief journey. But I also know that God's grace is sufficient for me. It has to be.

And so it goes for you.

Know this: In the face of hardship, pain, and suffering, the plan to take everything from you just so you would lay down and die did *not* succeed. I know it feels like it sometimes. And those feelings are very real. Mornings are still hard to bear for me. Something—or nothing—can trigger the pain. But know there will also be mystical, magical, miraculous moments. Moments that confirm there is so much more around us than what we can see. Moments that remind us of what is possible just beyond our human eyes. The devil underestimates the power of hope that still exists, even when love is broken or perverted. So despite our fears, our devastations, and our pain, we are still here and able to build a new life. Yes, grief means we move forward sometimes with a hole in our hearts the shape of the person or thing we lost. But it doesn't ever eliminate the purpose of our spirit. For me, I will die trying to guarantee that the twenty-seven hours I lovingly took to bring that baby girl into the world wasn't in vain. Hope prevails. The hope that lives in the eyes of children across three continents who have access to books and computers because of the work I do in Gabrielle's name. The hope of scholarship recipients who now get to grasp their futures. The hope of children who can dream big dreams regardless of their level of ability at the memorial Gabrielle's Playground. Despite my nightmares and the fight and faith it requires each day for me to literally get out of bed, I somehow have to go on. And you must too. Hope has long been the driver of day-to-day survival. I would hope as I woke up each morning that I would have the energy to make it through the day. I hoped that I would have the strength to stand before Gabrielle's murderer and point him out for the jury. And at some point along the way, when I could barely admit it to myself, I hoped to one day find love again.

To be clear: I always root for love. I always applaud love. But if in this moment of your life you aren't feeling loved or you're not even quite sure what love is, take a look at hope. Take a look at yourself and decide that you are going to bet on what you can imagine but can't touch. Write in your journal or murmur in your prayers things that are yet to be realized. Perhaps they seem impossible today, yet the mere fact you can utter or envision them means they can come true. Sometimes that's a new man, a new career, losing or gaining thirty pounds, and other times that's writing a book. Many times it will feel like the stuff of mere survival. Hope might just feel like:

> *I hope I can get in and out of the shower and to work today.*
> *I hope that I can sleep tonight because I haven't slept in a*
> *few nights.*
> *I hope that I can get through this conference call without them*
> *seeing my tearstained face.*

Those are some of the hopes I've held in dark days. If you give yourself no other gift, give yourself the gift of hope. We all face battles large and small every day. Be a hope warrior.

—8—

Look for *Your* Signs

March 2, 2018
In a gray wet morning darkness, I sit by my window to start
my morning rituals. I hope to see my cardinal, but as I open
the shades in the living room, I say in my heart, "I didn't get to
see her yesterday, so I really hope she comes today." I begin my
reading and whip my head to the window several times as I think
I hear the cardinal chirping in the distance. After several times
of anxiously scouring the landscape in the windy rain, bare trees,
evergreens, I see a beautiful burst of red. There she is, Gabi Bear
came to visit me.

One of my most powerful survival tactics, one I have long relied on and reached for within the first twenty-four hours of my daughter's murder, is writing. Writing has always been an important part of who I am, but this time, it saved my life. I remember listening to the *Hamilton* soundtrack over and over, with lyrics like "Why do you write like you're running out of time?" and "I'll write my way out." In those early days, my writing mostly took the form of the obituary, the eulogy, and then stream-of-consciousness journal entries. I took my Bible and journal outside at around 5 or 6 a.m. each morning and sat down. On that first day, within minutes, I heard a loud sound and then saw a splash of red flitting across the sky. I hadn't ever seen a cardinal in that space before.

It was like it was looking for me. I refer to the bird as "her" although I have since learned that the brilliant red cardinals are always male. Taking the privilege of assigning gender to animals is something that Gabrielle did often, and so I delight in imagining her feminine spirit in this bright and brilliant creature.

A deep love and connection created a pressure that filled my heart and body and was painfully familiar. Only one person could make me feel that way. The fact that the bird was so damn loud and vibrant struck me as familiar. My Gabrielle would not be silenced.

Every time I went outside, the bird would show up. I didn't have a bird feeder. There were no nests that I knew of. It could even be raining like the world was coming to an end, with no other birds in sight. This bird would always show up.

I was grateful for the sign. It drew me closer to the love I had thought was lost to me forever. I never loved anyone the way I loved Gabrielle. I remained in awe of every inch of her beautiful, soft, little body every day of her life. I treasured our bath-time songs and pool games. I cherished our nighttime song, which always ended with those tiny arms wrapped around my neck and her soft little kiss. She was flesh of my flesh, and she is still with me. I can feel it. The cardinal was my reminder of that. Without a doubt, the loss and suffering are crushing, but I'm so grateful that God chose to have her pass through me for her short journey. I cannot ever imagine a more perfect love. She was a physical manifestation of all of my hopes, dreams, brokenness, godliness. Every day without her is heartrending. But even with no sign of life other than the bending branches and blinding rain and wind, that bright burst of red assured me that she is somehow still here.

I was worried when I moved from that rental house shortly after her murder that the cardinal was a temporary fixture or that its visits were my desperate attempt to connect coincidence with divine providence. I tried to talk myself into preparing for the cardinal's exit. While I had seen the cardinal every day for those first few weeks, I wondered if I would ever see her again. I tried to prepare myself emotionally for the cardinal going away. During the final walk-through of the house, I cried. Outside it was raining sideways, which felt apropos. At one point, I looked out the window, and there she was. The bird landed, looked at me, and then flew away. I didn't want to leave.

The first morning at the new house, I stepped outside and started writing. Within five minutes, I looked up to see—you guessed it— a cardinal. She came by every day for a really, really long time. I needed to see it. The bird was a divine touchpoint for me. In the beginning, I'd cry every time the bird would leave. Later, I was grateful for the appearance and less tied to the length of its stay. I was comforted by its mere presence. Some days, as if in a demonstration of my faith, I would only hear it calling out in the distance. The sentiment of faith being the "substance of things hoped for, the evidence of things not seen," from Hebrews 11:1, was once again making itself plain.

The experience with my precious cardinal felt like a promise soaring down directly from heaven. And I listened. I'm still listening and looking for those miracle minutes. I couldn't help but begin reading a great deal about cardinals. I now know all of their calls at various times of the year. I also learned that throughout the ages, cardinals have served as spiritual reminders. Some cultures believe that when a cardinal lands in your yard, an angel is near. These birds can also remind you of a departed loved one and are known as the most notable of spiritual messengers.

When I first started sharing my story, I flew to Florida to speak at an executive Black women's conference. I'd attended this conference in the past, and there were easily six hundred women in attendance each year. This was unnerving, to say the least. I'd been asked to speak shortly after I founded Gabrielle's Wings, so I thought, *This is a good place for me to try out what it's going to be like to publicly share my story.* Before I spoke, I was sitting on a beach chair and talking with a friend about how hard it was going to be to talk to people about what happened. Lo and behold, a cardinal landed on the chair next to us.

The chair *next to us.*

I looked at my friend, and it was truly one of those "You saw that, right?" moments.

People often ask me what I think the cardinal means. They want to know what I believe Gabrielle might be saying to me. In the begin-ning, I'm sure it was "I'm still here. I know you don't understand, but I'm still here." Lately, however, it's been more about affirmation. She's saying, "You're on the right track. Keep going." Occasionally, when I'm struggling to move forward or in a heavy, grieving moment, it feels like she's saying, "Mommy, get up. Mommy, keep trying." The first day of what would have been the third grade for her, at 6 a.m., that bird started chirping. That was her. Urging me toward healing.

When your earth is rocked, it's like an emotional earthquake. You need to grab something. You're desperate for some evidence that there is life for you on the other side. Yes, the "thing" you grab will evolve over time. Early on, we are all reaching out for anything to steady us. Some of us grab something negative, like a bad relationship or too many cookies. Sometimes, grief can push us to start grasping for things that cannot be shaken from the earth; things that feel eternal. For me, that has always been nature. When my mother died, my fa-ther picked up my brother in Connecticut and came to DC to get me. It was a gorgeous day in February. The sky was crystal blue and the temperature was in the sixties. It may seem like a small thing, but that beautiful spring day in the midst of a Northeastern winter felt like a sign to me. A sign from my mother to be still and know that she was okay. These symbols—whether a bird or a surprising February sun—are precious reminders even as we reel from the initial impact. We might be saying, "I'm hungry. I'm thirsty. I'm hurting." But these symbols help us also say, "But the sky is still blue. And this pretty little bird is showing up every day, rain or shine. This bird is showing up and looking me in the eye and communicating that, oh yes, I'm still here. I'm still breathing."

Each symbol is a sign of life. Whether you've gone through a grief experience or not, if you believe God, the universe, or angels give you signs, then you will often find that those signs are affirmations that you're on the right path. They are reminders you are a divine being connected to other divine beings, and that while there may not be a reason for everything, while there may not be one plan, there is a course. My signs are like the mile markers I see when I drive into the mountains. There are signs informing me of the elevation, and there are others that warn about rocks and bears. When we have to reckon with our losses, we can relish the signs of familiarity and connection God provides. We are often looking for signs of hope, evidence that our faith is real. We've been shaken because we thought we knew what and who to trust. We thought we knew what love was, but then we were crushed. Signs give you back your confidence. They tell you that, actually, you weren't wrong. They affirm that you are on the right path. My friend often tells me, "Good things happen for a reason, horrific things like what you experienced just happen." That is so reassuring for all of us who torture ourselves with "what if" questions. Yes, this horrible thing happened, and *yet* you are still heading in a direction on this journey that will ultimately take you where you're supposed to go.

And know this: Your signs are *your* signs. They won't be the same as mine or anyone else's. Trust your gut enough to know that what you're seeing or hearing is real for you. That is what really matters. Nobody else has to get it. Nobody has to understand but you.

Since the early days, I've encountered Cardinal Lane signs in LA and daily visits by that bright and noisy little bird in three different homes. I've seen cardinals at hotels and on nature hikes. Close to home or hundreds of miles away. When I began traveling more frequently and for longer stints to Gabrielle's and my "happy place," in the Bahamas, there were no cardinals. But after persistent and noisy visits from a little bird, I did some research. A bunting bird. Part of the cardinal family. Their presence is known to speak of knowledge and intelligence, with an emphasis on utilizing your "voice" to "sing" your song. They are believed to teach you about the emotions that need to surface in order to heal. In the most unexpected places, my daughter's spirit and presence is affirmed.

The universe shows up shining brightly with unexpected signs in unexpected ways. Sometimes we arm ourselves for one type of battle and find out we need something completely different. I was terrified of spending my first Christmas without Gabrielle. There is nothing more quintessentially childhood than the joy of Christmas morning. I also celebrate my birthday right after Christmas. In December 2016, Gabrielle and I had celebrated at our "happy place" in the Bahamas. Now, less than a year later, I was trying to figure out how to reimagine that time. I prayed about what to do, and mission work came to my spirit. I was blessed to find an organization called Believers World Outreach. They do short-term missions around the world and had a holiday mission trip to Belize. My family was uncertain, and I was too. I was going alone with no information other than a Google search and a little research. I had confided in the president of the organization, a prayer warrior named Debbie. She assigned me to a roommate who is now like a true prayer sister to me, Katie. When I arrived in Belize coated in an armor of distance, I smiled. I talked to people. I engaged, but I feared "going there." However, although I couldn't imagine baring my soul during this most vulnerable time to strangers, I also couldn't imagine holding this dark pain and secret in all week.

The work was focused on children, and whatever icy and tough exterior I had planned to cling to in this unfamiliar territory was quickly melted away. The first day a little girl followed me everywhere. Her name was Lesbia and she had such a sweet spirit. She made a card for me that said, "I love you sooooooo much." That put chinks in the outer layer of my armor immediately. That was not only something Gabrielle always said, but Lesbia drew little hearts on the card that looked exactly like my baby's art. I felt something inside saying, *Check yourself. You have the right to protect yourself, but don't do it at the expense of missing a blessing.* I found out later that day that Lesbia and Gabrielle shared the exact same birthday. I couldn't imagine it was a coincidence.

So that night, as all of the missionaries gathered and shared why they had taken this trip, instead of my protected and safe planned answers, I went there. I stripped down from my armor and chose to bare my soul. The response was overwhelming. Thanks to a little girl, who I believe was sent by a little angel, I chose to check my armor at the door that night. Sometimes our signs will be little glimpses of possibility. They can remind us of who we are or challenge us to keep moving.

And sometimes in the most unexpected of places, through the holes in our armored hearts, we let down our guard enough to let the light in. If you open your heart and (literally) your eyes, you will find so many affirmative signs—both mini and miraculous—to be grateful for and to carry you through.

— 9 —

Return to Your Roots

It begins.
I hear them say in my sleep,
"It is what we've always done
and you have always made it through."
Capture
Fear
Injustice
Violence
The Middle Passage
Doing whatever love and desperation demand
necessary to protect and save and survive.

Loving and laughing and praying in ways that frighten
and confuse those who would mistake it with
Simple-ness.
Or Voodoo Magic
Or Ignorance
Those mere mortals who never understood
that the rhythm and movements which our hearts and souls cry out
Are from other skins
Under other suns
Sounds of drum and chant and melody preparing us for the ritual
  of battle

A fight for justice
A secret midnight path to freedom.

It is what we have always done.
Prayed.
Made a way out of no way.
Thanked Jesus anyhow.
Held on to the oral traditions and history
and passed it down
So the next generation would also know when their time came
Carrying close to breast and bone and spirit
that they too were descendants of royalty.
Of fighters.
Of survivors.
The "in spite" of
Those people who hope against hope . . .
Pain against pain . . .
Weakness against weakness . . .
Fear against fear . . .
Would do what we have always done.
Look to nature for our signs and songs
Look to God for our hope and mercy
Look to generations of ancestors
Possessing nothing and everything
Who walked as giants among simple and cowering men

We will do what we have always done.
Stand on the shoulders of a thousand soldiers.
Can't you hear them?
"My child, the time has come."
                    —"What We've Always Done" by Michelle Hord

Because I lost my mother suddenly in my twenties, people have always reached out to me when a moment of sudden loss—particularly the loss of a parent—arrives at their doorstep. They call or are directed to me by mutual friends as if I have a playbook. So I try to offer what I can. I challenge them to create their own playbook for coping. But I always say to them: Don't expect any one person in your life to have the answers you seek. No one has *your* playbook. But if you choose to be present each day and breathe through the waves of grief, answers will inevitably start to come. Yes, sometimes there isn't enough glue to put it all back together again. You can't go back. But you can go forward. One day, one hour, one second and millisecond at a time. One day you just might look back at the pieces of this picture you were forced to assemble out of haste and desperation and start to see the outline of a new horizon. When I speak to people, especially young women, about grief, I make sure they know that they can give themselves permission to grieve however they need to. It's my way of offering them some levity and letting them know that whatever they are going through, they are not alone. This—whatever this might be—has happened before. I know from experience how necessary it is that they keep their perspective and stay grounded while also feeling what they feel when they feel it.

I worshiped the ground my mother walked on. Her beauty was usually the first thing people noticed about her. And she was gorgeous! My grandfather called her Dolly her entire life because she looked just like a baby doll when she was born. Me, on the other hand? I was this lanky, awkward kid with this beautiful mother who often heard comments like "Your mom is beautiful. You don't look anything like her." Of course, as I've gotten older, I see more of her in the mirror than I ever thought possible. There is still some distance, though. She was truly the complete personification of womanhood to me. I often say that she was the type of woman who made people sit up straighter, made them want to smooth their blouses or skirts . . . without her ever saying a word.

My mother rarely cracked. She was the product of a different time and a different upbringing. I can count on one hand the number of times in my life I saw her cry. That's where we also differed.

Because I saw my mother as this beautiful woman who was so incredibly different from me, it became clear to me by the time I was a tween that my contortion into her mold was going to require a great deal of effort. While I rarely saw her cry, I was extremely empathic and emotional. I wore my feelings on the outside and struggled when others around me were more reserved. As a child, you don't necessarily understand that one way of being is not right or wrong. It's difficult to process that, from a generational and historical standpoint, Black people of my mother's era didn't always have access to therapy or the seeming "privilege" to stop and focus on feelings. In some ways, they learned that vulnerability could be dangerous, even fatal. Being perceived as too much of anything could draw unwanted attention, so trying to fit in as quietly as possible was the 1950s and '60s version of assimilation and survival. Maybe if *they* forgot you were there, maybe if *they* forgot you were different, undue or unwanted attention could be avoided. Attention that could cost jobs, friendships, peace, and, yes, sometimes even lives. It took some time for me to realize just how much of that factored into the way my mother moved through life. She was stoic, just as her mother was stoic. It never occurred to me that there was something unusual about her lack of emotion. In fact, it taught me that there was power in not wearing your emotions on your sleeve. So, although that wasn't my innate way of being, I learned that people shouldn't see me cry. That I needed to "buck up and be strong." I learned that compared to others, especially my ancestors, my struggles were small. It inadvertently also made me feel like my feelings were small too. Like many young women, my mother's image, both the physical and emotional demonstrations of it, was my first and most impactful model for what it meant to be Black and female. We were tall. People always saw us walk into a room, and it is an art form to be naturally noticed while fighting silently to not be seen. There was an understated strength and grace to my mother, and as I found myself trying to follow in her footsteps, I often stumbled and faltered. Inevitably, I found myself feeling frustrated or ashamed for falling short of her composure.

We create models and idols out of parents, lovers, sometimes even strangers on screens or in books. However, at some point, life requires us to create our own dance. The numbered footsteps of another will feel out of sequence until we are brave enough to choreograph our own. My mother was a painfully shy child. I shudder even writing things about her because she was so private. She also had a very small, close-knit community made up of family and one or two friends. For me, when I left home for college, I was freed for the first time to make up my own rules for living and loving and expressing. I didn't have a small, close-knit community. I delighted in knitting various and diverse communities together. I didn't follow convention. I played the drums on an all-male drumline. I wore my ponytail while carrying my sticks across campus in pink-and-green sorority sweats. I found my voice and ability to express it somewhere just beyond the hushed lines of prose scrawled in the dark of the bedroom of my youth. My womanhood was one of belly laughs and loud ugly cries and the big unorganized chaos of creativity and debate. There is no right or wrong or definitive rulebook on how you should walk your path, I learned. So if your steps are focused on the path or approval of others, you'll never fully actualize your *own* song or move freely with your own dance steps.

It wasn't until my mother died that I was truly left without a playbook. I had no map from her experience of dealing with the death of a parent, because that was not her journey. And it wasn't until I began to deal with my mother and grandmother's deaths, which happened within months of each other, that I began to understand that people emote differently and that it's all okay. I needed to reconcile what I could imitate and what I couldn't. Part of coming into my own was understanding that while my mother was stoic in her heroism, I might need to be something else.

WHEN I WAS growing up, I often struggled as this dramatic, expressive child to make sense of my emotional roller coaster. I believed that my mother operated on an emotional range from one to five, while I went from negative fifteen to three thousand. Through the lens of my teenage eyes, there were lows in my mind and heart that she couldn't possibly understand, and highs I experienced, risks and jumps I'd make, that she couldn't ever fathom. But over time, I began to see my mother as a constant reminder of levity and balance.

When I was in high school, we moved to Connecticut from Michigan halfway during my sophomore year. I was livid—a complete hell on wheels. What fifteen-year-old wants to leave their friends and the only place they've ever known to come somewhere they've only barely read about in geography class? In my frustration, I carved "I hate Connecticut" into my headboard. The only problem was that I spelled Connecticut wrong. My mother could have gotten angry and screamed and yelled at me, but she didn't. That wasn't her way. She may have wanted to lay me out, but she took a different approach. She simply looked at what I'd done and said, "You need to learn how to spell it before we get there."

So no, she may not have been a crier. But she taught me that cooler heads generally prevail. And even though I'm different in my expression of my emotions, I've never forgotten that either.

There was a social worker at Danbury High School, Mrs. Maureen Leopold, who knew just how hard I was taking the move. She understood that I was also dealing with all the completely normal challenges of having a developing teenage brain. I would often come to her office completely wrecked. I'd cry and talk about being homesick; how I didn't have any friends. Her words in response have never left me:

"Michelle, it's okay. Everyone gets their crazy half hour."

It is one of the most impactful and freeing things anyone has ever said to me. Many adults and children aren't given permission to be what and where they are in any given moment. We aren't allowed to be sad. We likely weren't even asking to be sad forever, but it can be painful to feel as though you cannot feel sad or angry or whatever might be coming up for you in that moment. Our emotions should never be an excuse for harming someone else or for other types of negative or damaging behavior; in truth, if we are simply allowed to feel our feelings in an environment and with people who are truly safe, we are less likely to get to the point of danger or despair. So I often quote Mrs. Leopold's wise expression. It is empowering. It is an invitation. Yes, take the time you need. Shut the door. Pull the covers over your head. And then, when you're done, wipe your face and smooth your hair and get back into the game.

Like many women, I had to figure out what parts of my mother, her way of being, were a part of me and what pieces I was going to have to build on my own. My life experiences required that. When I lost my mother, yes, I was sad and angry, but there was also an urgency to learn from it. At the time of her death at fifty years old, my mother was perfectly healthy, but she was also dealing with the hardest thing in her life—the potential loss of her own mother. And she didn't have the language or the therapeutic support to know what and how to deal with that. Her village was much smaller than mine. As I began to try to understand cerebral aneurysms more, I discovered that holding in some of those strong emotions could have contributed to one. And I learned that my being more free to express my emotions also meant that I could release those feelings from my body that so many Black and brown women of previous generations were forced to hold in. And these same women were twice as likely to have a brain aneurysm than white women. So if my grief over my mother taught me anything, it was that I needed to build a support system and have the courage to have my crazy half hours, when necessary. I was going to have to give my grief a voice—to scream it aloud—in order to survive. Part of coming to terms with what our parents gave us, versus what they lacked, is acknowledging that they are who they are, and they did what they could with what they had. But it also may mean embracing the fact that because you have a different life experience, you have more access to resources, and you don't have to make their same mistakes.

AS I ALLUDED to earlier, some of the differences between me and my mother were just a function of being born in different time periods and having different childhoods. One of seven, my mom grew up in a small rural Southern Illinois community called Pinkstaff, on a country dirt road. I jokingly sometimes referred to her as the Black Sandra Dee because she never drank or swore. But she and my father had created a different life for my brother and me. Together they took their collective small-town Midwest experiences and fashioned the best possible version of the American dream available for their children.

My dad, Noel Edward Hord, was the fourth child out of five kids. He was named after his father, and the tradition has continued with my brother and my nephew. They all have different middle names, which has become a way to pass down legacy while also allowing each generation to create its own. My dad was the only one in his family who didn't graduate first or with high honors in his class in high school. He also often jokes that he would come into a classroom and the teacher would say, "Oh, you're Katherine's brother. We know what you're going to do." And he'd say, "Let's wait and see!"

He flunked out of college, not because he wasn't smart, but more because his motivations were different. He'd just married my mother, who was three years older than him, and for a period of time, he wasn't working. Nevertheless, every morning he'd get up when she did, searching the papers for work, because he refused to be sitting in the house by himself when his woman was out there working. That was the beginning of his American dream story.

Dad got his first job as a stock person at Ben Becker Shoe Company, a popular fine shoe shop owned by a white man named Herman Becker in Terre Haute, Indiana. It was the late 1960s and a big deal for a Black man to even be working in a store that mostly served white clientele. He started as a stock boy and was soon promoted to a sales role, but only within the men's department. The racial prejudices of the day made it controversial for him to even touch a white woman's feet. What they didn't count on was just how popular my dad was at the newly integrated high school in the city. All of the white girls from his school would come into the store while he was working in the back, stocking shoes, and say, "Can Noel wait on us?" At some point, they had to allow him to move up into a sales position outside of just men's shoes, so he could also serve women and children customers. In fact, he was the first Black salesperson in the town. With that one opportunity, he climbed the corporate ladder and changed the trajectory of his and our lives. We went from living in a very modest apartment to a modest house to a stately home in one of the wealthiest counties in the country. We went from our small community of family and friends to my father appearing in *Ebony*, *Jet*, and *Black Enterprise* magazines. From hard-earned trips to Disney World to vacations in Bermuda by the time I left for college. By the 1990s, after lots of hard work and perseverance, my father had become the president and chief operating officer of the multimillion-dollar company Nine West, the largest non-athletic shoe company in the US at that time.

I grew up with this larger-than-life, American dream story. One that I know many people can't fathom. And I'm grateful that my parents always held the expectation that my brother and I would be required to work just as hard as they did. It was that old, Black parent adage of "God bless the child that's got his own." But I'm grateful because it taught me about hard work and endurance. I knew how to climb because I'd watched my father do it.

My mother, on the other hand, was not loud or verbose, but her presence roared. She taught me different lessons. In many ways, I worshiped her. We had such an incredible bond. It was so intense, in fact, that I was told that she left the hospital early after giving birth to my brother—something that just didn't happen back then—because she was worried about me being away from her. I was safe, of course. My maternal grandmother had come to stay with us, whom I also adored. But we were so attached to each other.

Mom was an elementary schoolteacher but stayed home with me until I was five years old. And when I left home for elementary school, she moved me from our neighborhood school to the school where she taught. Probably because she wasn't satisfied with the school and also because of our attachment to each other. My dad often jokes about my first time getting on the bus for school and how my mom followed the bus all the way to school, while I sat in the back window and waved at her.

In short, my mom was everything. She was my protector. I was sensitive and shy, and it was "behind her skirt" that I found a safe place to cry and hide.

I eventually grew out of my shy phase as a child, becoming an outgoing teenager and young adult. I started playing the drums only because when I asked about it, the band director didn't think it was something for girls to do. I never learned how to play basketball because, due to my height, my whole life people would ask me if I did. There has always been this "rebel without a pause" part of my personality. My defiant faith was just straight-up defiance for a long time! But my rebellion was kept in check because the worst thing in the world I could hear was my mother saying, "I'm disappointed." That was a dagger to the heart. So yes, I snuck and wore makeup in middle school and got in trouble when I forgot to take it off, but it was all so benign. I knew she loved me, but I was always seeking my mother's approval.

This is why, as a young woman, not being like her and wanting to please her were very complicated for me. I thought the world revolved around her—and my world certainly did. It is also why I carried such an enormous fear of her dying. I remember several times, as both a child and young adult, dreaming that she would die. When I read stories that involved losing one's mother, they shook me to my core. In those panicked late-night terrors, I'd rush into the room she and my father shared to ensure she was still breathing.

I was never able to shake those awful nightmares. I sometimes wonder if there was a part of my spirit that knew she would leave us too soon. It was as if my spiritual self was trying to prepare my human self for an inevitable yet unimaginable loss at a fairly early age. There was a kind of foreshadowing in my subconscious that fueled the dreams I would have. I'm aware that, for some, that doesn't make sense. But based on what experience has taught me, I believe there was something in my body that sensed a shift coming, even when I didn't know it intellectually, and kept me close to her as a result.

In truth, the hardest part of watching my grandmother get sick was processing the impact her illness was having on my mother as a caregiver and daughter. It felt surreal. I watched my mother experience my worst nightmare, losing her mother, and that prompted me to stick even closer to her. I flew to be with my mother as my grandmother went through chemo. I was a twenty-three-year-old producer still living in Washington, DC, and still attached to my Howard University "umbilical cord" of friends and surroundings. My parents had moved to Ohio from Connecticut that year. I would meet my mom in Houston, where her oldest sister lived and where my grandmother would convalesce while going through chemo and surgery at MD Anderson. One of my dear college friends, Camille, who later became the first Black female plastic surgeon in the state of Texas, was a young, exhausted medical school resident at the time. She always found time, though, to research my grandmother's doctors and offer any information she could to my mom and our family.

I sent my mom a card two days before she died. We never got a chance to talk about it, but the card basically said, "I can't imagine what it's like dealing with an aging parent. I'm here for you and I love you." I was so afraid that she would leave, so I made sure that I always let her know that I would be there for her. So imagine getting that call from my dad: "Your mother's gone." My world shattered. My worst nightmare had come to pass. The shock to our family and community of losing my mother so suddenly, as she and my dad became empty nesters and started a new life in Ohio, was staggering. Even after she died, furniture and fixtures she had ordered for their new house continued to arrive. A reminder of a *before* that had disappeared before our eyes.

I'd just come into my womanhood when I lost my mom to a cerebral aneurysm. We'd only recently gotten to the point of being comfortable having adult conversations. My time with her by my grandmother's side allowed me to be there for her for the first time as a woman versus as her child.

After she died, I thought about the many times I called home from college or my first apartment distraught by a dream where I'd lost her.

Her response was classic and cool: "Girl, I'm not going anywhere."

But she did.

She was perfectly healthy, and by the time I was twenty-four, she was gone.

Within a week of my mother dying, I had one of those dreams again that didn't feel like a dream. She was wearing her University of Michigan nightgown that, though frayed and in pieces, I still have to this day. In the dream she said, "It feels so good to be home."

I asked, "Why did you leave me?"

She responded, "I had to go, but you have everything you need."

I wanted to believe her when she said that I had everything I needed, but I didn't understand what that meant exactly. I couldn't see it and so I disagreed. "What do you mean, Mom? I'm twenty-four years old. I have to deal with your forty-seven-year-old husband and your twenty-one-year-old son. I have to watch your mother die. I don't know how to handle this. I don't even know how you make your pot roast. I literally don't have everything I need."

But when I lost Gabrielle, I understood what she meant. First, I'm so grateful my mother did not have to live through this horrible thing happening to her grandchild, to her daughter. I also found comfort in imagining, in my mortal mind, their meeting at the gates of Glory, having met there in the spirit before Gabrielle was sent to me. I imagined my mother's open arms and precious smile, taking my sweet girl in.

In that dream, so long ago, my mother was telling me that the courage and resilience I needed would kick in, if I allowed it to. She didn't say it would be pretty. We don't always get it right the first time. We never know what life is going to hand us, but we need to believe that we have the stuff we need to work it out when "it" comes. One of my mother's favorite songs from *The Wiz* was "If You Believe," sung by Lena Horne. She sings, "If you believe/within your heart you'll know/that no one can change/the path that you must go." I desperately needed to believe in myself at certain times in my life, and I think that's the message of that dream. Yes, when the circumstance calls for it, I will have everything I need. It's like opening a puzzle and trying to figure out what to do with all the pieces. In my journey, there have been times when I've seen the picture on the box cover clearly and then found it impossible to assemble the puzzle from the splintered pieces on the floor. There are other times that the gaps between the pieces are so vast that it feels like I will never begin to fill in the empty spaces. But somehow, when everything is "put together," the composite of my experiences enables me to do whatever it is I'm supposed to do in this world.

Maybe God allows signs to come our way in order to help ease us through hardship when it comes into our lives. Maybe these moments are seeds of awareness that will eventually flower. Or maybe some of us just manifest our lives in a way that we become sharper and more attuned to spiritual things. Regardless, I've learned to watch and listen. In the same way that my cardinal visits to offer me affirmation in the voice and spirit of Gabrielle, my mother has revealed herself many times over the years.

Shortly after my mother's death, Dorothy Daniels, the mother of four of my dearest friends, whom I met at Howard University, wrote me a letter. She had never even met my mom but began actively praying and fasting for the right words to share with me. What came out was a letter written in first person as if my mother had written it. It sounded just like my mom. The phrasing, word choice, shared Bible verses, everything! I was stunned. There are times in your life—especially in your twenties—when you don't know what you need until you need it. It's such a blessing to have people who have the audacity to say, "I'm not asking you. I'm telling you that I'm here. I'm standing in the gap right now." Having never met my mother, but having some similarities in terms of faith, Mrs. Daniels had the nerve and audacity to fast and pray for two or three days and then write in first person to someone else's child. She referenced Philippians 4:13—"I can do all things through Christ who strengthens me"—and it was as if she'd truly embodied my mother.

Mrs. Daniels provided me with what I needed to hear in that moment. This was a woman who was the mother of children my age and who had her own mother still. I'm sure she couldn't imagine losing her mom at my tender age. So she stepped in and served me in the only way she knew how, through a mother's prayers and love. At one point, she even moved in with me for a while. She was truly a mother figure too. Asking all the invasive questions a mom would ask.

"Is the water hot enough when you're washing your face?"

"Why aren't you separating these clothes before you wash them?"

"Are you getting enough vegetables? Are you constipated?"

One of the most powerful messages in Mrs. Daniels's letter was that my mother would send people to intercede on her behalf. I started looking for the signs, and finding them.

Like the time I was at the hairdresser sitting next to an older Black woman who was about the age my mother would have been. My stylist asked me what kind of soap I used on my face, and I said, "I use whatever is handy." Out of nowhere, the elder said, "You are too old to not use a real facial cleanser and moisturizer on your face!" I was so tickled that my mother's words and voice had just left that woman's mouth.

Okay, Mom, I get it. I'll buy some Cetaphil. I'll put the generic soap down!

Then there was the time when Gabrielle was one and a half and able to stand on her own just enough to scare me. I would look on the baby monitor and she'd be standing up in her crib, staring at my mother's rocking chair that I kept in her room. She'd stand there and just babble her little head off. Hank and I would always say that she's talking to my mom, and I believe she was.

Historically, Black mothers do not prepare their children for a buffet of acceptance and tolerance. They prepare us for war. And my mother equipped me for whatever was going to come my way. That letter Mrs. Daniels sent to me was certainly an "I love you," but it was also provision; those words gave me tools. Through that letter, I could feel my mother saying, "Listen, here's the battle plan. This is what you need, and you're going to be okay."

I think we all have the ability to see the unseen if we're open to it. All of these moments are like portals, opening me up to looking for the divine. Some days, I think these early "signs and wonders" were my mom's way of saying "I need you to be able to pay attention to the divine because in a few years you're going to need to be able to do this in a completely different way. It's going to save your life."

Whether it's a cardinal in a tree outside your window or intercession from another person, there's always a chance for divine intervention in your circumstances. Will these huge events happen every single moment of every day? No. But I do believe that we have opportunities every day to touch the divine; to be affirmed and encouraged. We won't see or hear them all. Sometimes our lives will be too chaotic and we'll miss them. But they are there. That's why taking a minute to stand still, to watch and listen, is so critical. Take moments of solitude, even brief ones, to hear what you need to hear. Even as I sit here quietly and alone with my fingers touching the keyboard, a butterfly is dancing by my window in the sun.

Even if the concept of God is foreign to you or you are simply not a believer, it's okay to see these as signs from a universe that we are all connected to in some way. I've had moments when I've been in need and a soft breeze brushed against my arm. My response? "Okay, God." Or there have been times when I'm thinking about Gabrielle and I'll hear the cardinal chirp. I just say, "Okay, Gabi Bear." It takes work to find ways to create enough quiet in your brain. Enough space to listen to your own heart and intentions. If we are willing to imagine that our hearts and spirits are connected to other hearts and spirits, then it's only a short leap to embracing these symbols and signs as another form of communication.

Hold them as affirmations and use them to help you move through your grief at a pace that feels right to you. These symbols, no matter their source, do affirm us. We just have to receive them as such.

Being able to see things in this way also serves the collective. We grapple with our demons as individuals, but there is also such a thing as collective war when whole groups of people mourn a person or tragic event. When people gather and bring food because it is something, maybe even the only thing, they can do. We each experience struggle in our own ways, but from job loss to death we are rarely alone in the aftermath of pain—what happens to us has an impact on others. That means that when others are lifted up, that can have an impact on us too. The common and defining emotions and life experiences—love, loss, partnering, parenting, success and failure of all kinds—are the things that have a human shorthand. If we are open to the idea that we are all connected at the level of heart and spirit, we can use that energy to fuel kindness and service. I've had the experience of being in an airport and watching a young mom struggle with carrying a stroller, baby, and other mommy accessories and being able to experience the joy of saying, "Hey, I got you. I know what you're dealing with. Let me get the stroller for you." Embracing these moments of spiritual communication, even in the midst of our grief, is very important in a world where the darkness is obvious and the light is not.

Leaning in to these moments means having an expectation of light wherever you go. And yes, it could just be a moment. The brevity doesn't matter. Don't let those little moments slip by you. They are the root of our humanity and the thing that stitches us all together.

I won't even pretend to know how it all works, but I do know that

Gabrielle, my mother, and her mother are all here. They are close to me. They are rooting for me, the last earthly link in our female family chain. In moments of difficulty or indecision, I hear the song of a cardinal or see a flutter of a butterfly's wings and I understand that I am supported and surrounded by love.

Everyone's experiences are different. But pay attention when you feel a kindred spirit after meeting someone for the first time. Tune in when something just falls in your lap. If you can stretch your imagination away from labeling it as mystical and simply enjoy a moment of grace and majesty, then you'll be able to experience even a strong breeze as an affirmation of something divine. These kinds of signs are gateways of hope as we navigate the grief process. I've found comfort in them. It isn't always literal handwriting on a wall, but it is a way the universe affirms life is still here, opportunities for abundant living are still available, and there is a cloud of witnesses continuing to root for and protect you. When you need that strength, the reminder that there's more to this life, those signs are there for you. They are symbols of hope declaring, "Yes, you can. You are all right. It may not be easy, but you have everything you need."

— 10 —

Reimagine Your Road

Surviving traumatic events often means finding a way to see old things in a new light. Other times it means finding peace and meaning in new things. This journey is really about what you leave behind and what you bring with you.

I have attended the same church (Grace Baptist Church) since before I lost Gabrielle. Some things you have to take with you. Some things you have to retrieve from the embers of your scorched life and hold on to for dear life. My church is one of those things. The church steps are the same ones we carried Gabrielle up when she was a baby. The rocky parking lot adjacent to the church is where we would sometimes park. Gabrielle liked to pretend we were walking on the moon and would make dramatic and large steps in her patent leather Mary Janes. I half scolded and half laughed as I did what any self-respecting Black mama would do—admonished her not to scuff them.

Gabrielle's paternal grandmother used to go to church with us every Sunday. In fact, she spent most weekends with us. She was decades older than me but seemingly had Gabrielle's boundless energy and enthusiasm for life. Every week, there we were, three generations of women from different roots but the same soil, mounting those steps. Gabrielle's last caregiver is also a deacon at our church and had just begun talking to Gabrielle about getting baptized. One evening, before bed, Gabrielle beckoned me with a whisper. She said, "Mommy, I asked

Jesus into my heart, but don't tell Grandma because she will get too excited."

Everything about that church changed in our *after*. The sanctuary became the last place I would see and touch Gabrielle's body, in the small white casket with little pink flowers. I returned to church for the first time weeks after that awful day. I sat with my father on Father's Day and was so anxious, I could barely sit still in the hard, wooden pew. I felt suffocated from the eyes and attention and love. It was too soon, I suppose. Too much light on the darkness of my existence. The elders at the church rallied around me on Gabrielle's behalf, yet their efforts did not penetrate. All that time I felt the isolation and solitary grief of a lone survivor. Even with everyone around me, I felt alone.

Until I saw Mrs. White again for the first time at Hank's sentencing. There she was, frail and shaking. Standing up not for her son, but for her only beloved grandbaby. During the years we were estranged—a precaution during the criminal trial—we sent birthday, Mother's Day, and Christmas gifts. We wrote notes and sent cards to each other. Letters with words that couldn't articulate or attach to the deep pain we both were feeling. I ached knowing this wonderful woman was left to wrestle demons even more complicated than my own. She was loving enough to understand why I had to keep my distance.

Reconnecting wasn't easy, but it was important to me. So slowly after the sentencing, I began to reach out to her. Short dinners and acts of kindness. Ways to connect but not dwell too deeply or for too long on our shared grief and trauma.

Like me, Mrs. White had also lost her mother. She'd lost hers as a toddler. It was always clear to me that this was part of the reason she made such a tremendous effort to be there for me as a mother, even though she knew she could never replace mine. She was an extraordinary grandmother and loved Gabrielle so much. In my dark moments in the middle of the night, if I try to imagine what could possibly be worse than losing a child the way I did, I imagine the dark abyss of my only child doing something so horrible to my only grandchild.

It's certainly complicated, but I do see her in a similar place to the one I'm in. The foundation of everything we had is gone and corrupted.

And yet, there are reminders of before. Seeing her requires me to drive past the same apartment building that I've driven past for the last twenty years. The place where I would drop off and pick up my baby in her stroller and get her grandma's account of the day. The two-year period of time between the crime and the sentencing felt like forever, and then no time at all when we reconnected. I had always wanted her in my life, but I had to be cautious during the legal proceedings. One Sunday after the sentencing, I invited her to come back to church with me. With all the COVID-19 precautions in place, my church congregation hadn't gathered in months. Pastor Richardson offered an outside "socially distanced" service from our cars. It was the sanctified version of an old drive-in. I decided to invite Mrs. White to attend, and she gratefully accepted the offer.

So, there we were. In front of the church. Together in our *yet*. It was the first time she had been in that space since the funeral. Gabrielle's former nanny saw us and despite social distancing rules gave us both huge hugs. Standing there was one of the church elders who had tried to take Hank on as his own son, and he approached us with love in his eyes. We were beckoned toward the front of the crowd who had left their cars, masked, to be closer to the music and the message. They stood there, testifying in the streets, and calling us forward so the pastor could see us. We stood side by side to hear Pastor Richardson speak.

It's incredibly difficult to mine the pieces of your *before* to know what should go with you into your *yet* and *after* seasons. At the end of the day, you should listen to your heart. I walked into that church parking lot with trepidation, but not an expectation. When the old story goes away and you have a new chapter of your life to write, you must literally embrace the blank pages. And even though you may be inclined to write in your old style or revisit some of your old characters, the story really is all new. I did not know what to expect when I reconnected with Mrs. White. I did not know how it would feel. I just knew that something deep down in my bones said, "Call her."

It's right for me to honor this other most important person in my baby's life. To honor the fact that we are two survivors of a war that no one else participated in, and that part of my healing, part of me continuing into *after*, was going to require me to face every aspect of my *before* and declare myself a winner to everything that had tried to destroy me.

Part of putting a new life together with disparate puzzle pieces is admitting that the gaps are okay. As you ready yourself to move into your *yet*, you may need to rewrite or reclaim pieces from your *before*. That is your right. That is your choice. For me, I chose not to punish my former mother-in-law, or frankly myself, by walking away from her. This was a relationship that was important to me not only because of what she meant to Gabrielle, but because of what she meant to me. As I told her at one point when she questioned our reconnecting, "Hank has taken enough away from us. He doesn't get to take us away from each other too."

Facing and even embracing parts of your *before* allows you to see just how much you've grown, but it also helps you clearly see what and who you need to take with you into the future. Will my relationship with Mrs. White ever look like it used to? No, because the center of our collective joy was Gabrielle. Our relationship is now filled with these potholes. We're both always standing on the other side of that chasm, but for me, it's worth it to still stand there. It doesn't always feel good. I don't have a storybook, romantic ending about us being closer now than ever before. But because of who we are to each other and what we have both endured, I needed to bring her with me into my next chapter.

At the end of the songs and praise, the pastor asked those still in their cars to blast their horns for five minutes. He asked them to blast their horns in testimony. All of us who had lost jobs, who had faced illnesses, who were living in fear or uncertainty in the middle of the unexpected and unpredictable pandemic, were able to bear witness. We were still here. We could make a joyful noise and declare that the worst had come, and it had not silenced us. The people in all those cars blasted their horns to say in spite of . . . nevertheless . . . yet. And we stood there, resolute, two survivors of evil's plot. We raised our hands and let the tears fall. Somehow, we found gratitude and reconciliation more powerful than even the pain or regret. Above the sound of the horns, my pastor repeated this declaration over and over again: "I am still here!" I say it with him—defiantly—in my heart.

I am still here.

Lift your eyes and heart and listen for your music, my friend.

You are still here too.

Here may look different than you ever imagined, but there are still tears and testimony, choirs and choreography.

The universe will affirm your existence if you can quiet your pain and focus on your promise long enough to listen.

Listen and look for the signs.

— 11 —

Declare a Defiant Faith

July 16, 2017
I got the urn today. It is a seashell and looks like something you
would pass at Disneyland while waiting for the Ariel ride. My
whole life, all my hopes and dreams, every nervous and sorrowful
piece of my spirit, is represented in those ashes. How will God make
beauty from my ashes? If I wait till my last breath, my miracle
won't happen. My child is not coming back. Right now, it feels like
my throat is closing. I want to vomit. I'm so sad, so angry, so scared,
so bitter. I have faith, but I am struggling to hold on to hope.

We live so often with the expectation of understanding. We have access to so many answers, so many facts right at our fingertips. There has to be a YouTube video or Google search that covers everything, right? Wrong. The first step in surviving, in just staying afloat, was to admit that everything that had kept me buoyant and stable was gone. I had to release the expectation of ever having an explanation for what happened to my life and to my baby. The ship was wrecked. I had to choose to defiantly declare my faith even when there was no explanation. My hungry searches for some guidance filled my early days and nights after her murder. If I was going to be able to still stand, I needed to find my emotional kickstand to prop me up.

So this is spiritual warfare?

The answer was clear. There are no rationalizations and there is no reconciling. And when I finally realized that, I said to myself: *I will be damned if the devil wins.* There was nothing that could have ripped me to shreds, filled me with fear and betrayal, upended my worst nightmares like what happened to me. In that moment, my spirit told me that whatever I was supposed to do in the world, whatever path I was perhaps unknowingly on, was too important to let evil conquer me.

So I made some clear decisions about how to proceed. One, I was not going to allow my daughter to be a tabloid story. I would ensure that the legacy of service in her name would be bigger than what happened to her. Two, I would hold on to my hope, however thin, like my life depended on it. Because it did. It still does.

There it is again: hope.

Hope meant that I would not be felled. I was not going to let this heavy, awful thing take me out. For someone who always wanted to have a child, who was always told perhaps she couldn't, who had a flawless pregnancy and gave birth to this beautiful, bright child, and who was on the precipice of a whole new chapter of her life when all of it was taken away, there was something in me that needed to harden like steel to survive. Gabrielle was killed when I was forty-seven, not twenty-seven. I may adopt, but I will not physically be able to give birth to a child again. So losing her in this way felt like a cutting off every connection to my dreams of motherhood. There was no road back. My faith had to be defiant in the face of that nightmare. My hope had to be in a "stronghold in times of trouble" and had to be the driver of my faith.

> Now faith is the substance of things hoped for,
> the evidence of things not seen.
> —Hebrews 11:1 (NIV)

Faith is something you cannot see. It's not visible but you believe it is there. Faith is a dream that perhaps is not realistically actionable, but you believe it can happen. We can have faith in ourselves. We can have faith in a God. We can have faith in a relationship. In whatever form, faith is a covenant between you and another entity or the universe that says, "even when I can't see it, I'm going to believe it's possible." Perhaps the first steps of healing, the first thing you can truly do as you declare your *yet*, is to make the declaration that your past is real and true and irrevocable—*and* there are new truths for you to grasp and find. You don't have to name or claim them in that moment. That takes time. However, having the courage to imagine something else will keep you slowly stumbling toward that light.

Yet is a pivot. It connects your known past with the unknown future. Accepting that your life *before* has been forever changed gives you the opportunity to then lean in to *yet*.

Yet, I will be successful.
Yet, I will find love.
Yet, I will somehow heal after this tragedy.
Yet, I can have a wonderful life even if it doesn't look like
    I expected.

Harnessing the power of your *yet* gives you the ability to harness your internal strength to take back your narrative. This is especially true as you perhaps face external circumstances you cannot control.

It's a challenge to think about all the moments that make up our *before* life, particularly in a relationship. With our partners, we hold moments in pregnancy, labor, and childbirth. There are funny moments. Embarrassing moments. Terrifying moments. Moments with sick babies who aren't as sick as we feared they are. We look to our partners to help us account our history. They are also documenting our life experiences and who we are alongside them.

And when you have a child, it's so easy to be distracted by the doing that you sometimes don't take a step back to watch what's happening. Those wonderful, precious, golden little moments as your child grows and begins to discover the world around them can be lost without a mate who can also mentally and emotionally record them. So there was something incredibly lonely about the experience I went through. There is still no one who can truly walk this walk wearing my shoes. I am a parent of a murdered child, without the ability to even lean on the other parent for support, comfort, or even those closely held memories. I am alone with borrowed love and borrowed families and borrowed moments of intimacy and belonging. This is the reality. It is a solitary grief, and this is where that defiant faith holds me up.

When we can't lean on the love of family and friends, we can carry a staff of faith that props us up. That staff tells us that we have in our hands what we need to face the unknown and rocky terrain. It offers us protection and the security of something we can touch and feel. This defiant faith reminds us of who we are and Whose we are, when we lose our way.

My father often says he's so grateful for my faith and my fight. That about sums up what I think is necessary to survive this kind of overwhelming grief. It is a fighting faith. It is not passive. It stands in front of me and defends me. It keeps me from giving up, giving in, and feeling sorry for myself in those dark moments. It roots me on and challenges me to own what I can and hold on despite the unknown. It is not an "I'm going to sit here and wait for a sign" faith. It's an "I've got the matches and I'm burning the damn bush myself" faith. It is my cornerstone.

Please indulge the English/journalism major in me for a moment. Defiance is defined as a boldness, a resistance, and the ability to challenge. My defiant faith says that despite what is obvious, I am going to hold on to what I've always held on to with the assurance that it will eventually be what I know it to be. It says that my insurance policy will eventually pay out. I may not understand how I got here or where I'm going, but there is still a vehicle guiding me along. When we think of a fight, a myriad of things come to mind. It can be something violent or simply an ongoing conflict or feeling of aggression. When I consider faith and fight together, I think of activity and movement. There are times when we can be graceful and defiant. When we hold fast and "shall not be moved." When our mere presence or expression tells the story. And there are the other times. Times when we have to fight like hell. When that fight isn't pretty or planned, scripted or controlled. When advocating for your needs is perceived as rebellion. When your fighting words frighten or confuse people. Guess what? That's okay too. Honestly, I believe you need both kinds of fight. Overcoming often requires both.

You need those times when you can hold on to your spiritual ground-ing with confidence despite what you see. Those are the times when you simply trust that the sun will still rise tomorrow. And yet, there are also times when all you have is your ability to physically dog-paddle through crashing waves. In those instances, mere survival seems almost impossible. You take in air and water and choke it back and somehow still poke your head above the raging sea. This is when you consciously choose to still show up. The grace of defiant faith requires that fight. It's the backbone of it. When your faith becomes a weapon, you can wield it deftly against anything that tries to take you under.

Defiant faith can be quiet. It can also roar. It might look like days when you get up, get dressed, and show up for other people. It might look like staying in bed all day and resting your heart and body. Trust yourself. Trust the God you're tethered to. If you don't have a spiritual belief, trust that the sun will rise every day despite the day you had be-fore. Trust that the trees will still move in a slow waltz to the wind, the birds will still soar across the sky, and life will continue to happen. Be brave enough to keep going, even when you don't know where your next steps will take you. It doesn't matter how you stand or sit, what you say or do, just keep going. Your *yet* may be just around the corner.

— 12 —

Accept What Was Lost

"When I let go of what I am, I become what I might be."
—Lao Tzu

Shimmer was the name Gabrielle gave the sedan I leased when she was five years old. She held the honor of naming any and everything in our house—mostly inanimate objects. There was the exception, of course. She named her betta fish *Rainbow Feathers*. More often than not, though, it was things, like my car, that she named. It was precious and hilarious. I often joked among friends that my car had been bequeathed a stripper's name.

I generally don't hold huge connections to material things. I guess I can attribute that to how I was raised. As the old folks used to say, I come from "good stock." Hardworking ancestors who made their way up from slavery, to the Midwest of America. I was born to Midwestern parents who created the American dream for my brother and me right before our eyes; yet they taught us to celebrate the rewards of hard work versus the trappings of material spoils. So "things" were never a priority. However, objects that take on the shape of precious memories are something else entirely. Those connections are much more about what is associated with the object than what the actual object happens to be.

Shimmer was the car that carried Gabrielle and me to and from soccer practices and Girl Scout meetings. It was the car that helped me do drop-offs and pick-ups from Gabrielle's elementary school. The car where she sat and questioned me about divorce and shared her feelings. We sang songs together there. Discussed the never-to-be new décor and paint of our house together. I've been grateful to find that many of Gabrielle's videos and selfies were recorded there in the backseat where she reigned.

After Gabrielle was murdered, a friend had the car washed and carefully detailed. Gabrielle's car seat was gone. Given where my mind-set was at the time, it is entirely possible that I requested this of her. Yet, after she had painstakingly done it, I collapsed at another sign that my life was forever changed.

There were times in those early months after I lost Gabrielle when I would suddenly feel her presence while alone in the car. There is this familiar pressure upon my chest that feels full of a love and life, almost too heavy for me to endure. I would often look in the rearview mirror and place my hand where a car seat holding my precious girl should have been. The feeling was meditative. Touching the smooth leather that once held her precious body, along with everything from Cheerios to art supplies in the cracks and crevices, soothed me in a way.

My car lease ended several months after her murder and I had another hard decision to make. A decision that, either way, would be another admission of her absence. Another way I would be forced to publicly acknowledge that my world would never be the same. I remember planning methodically for the day when I would turn the car in to the dealership. Yet when that sunny but frigid morning arrived, it was impossible. Less than a mile from the dealership I sat frozen and hysterical in a bank parking lot unable and unwilling to give another outward sign of loss. Another thing I would have to give up. Another tangible object that I could silently share my memories with was being pulled from my hands and my possession.

I folded that day. Letting go of the car was too much, and the subsequent emotions that overwhelmed me were tough to process. I wanted to move forward but struggled to do so. But through it all, I had a simple but significant revelation: Letting go is hard.

It isn't always about an object. It is nearly always about the emotions attached to it. Whether it was that luxury sedan or later the clothes and toys that once belonged to my daughter, I've been faced with letting go over and over again. This is likely true for you too, friend. It is challenging when we are forced to let go of physical things and places: wedding bands, a pre-pregnancy figure, old jobs. Other times we are letting go of emotional things: love, peace of mind, status, freedom.

Sometimes we can let go of things and not look back; we can be content with the memory. But other times, in the moment of release it doesn't matter to us how much the item/person/feeling costs. It doesn't matter whether or not we still want to hold on to the idea, dream, or feeling that brought us there to begin with. It only matters that the object or the emotions generated by the object are still very much a part of us. Sometimes, we are connected to what or who we lost through a physical or symbolic portal; shutting that portal down can feel like opening an even deeper chasm of emptiness and despair. And yet, in some cases, we still must do it. The venerable advice columnist Ann Landers once said, "Some people believe holding on and hanging in there are signs of great strength. However, there are times when it takes much more strength to know when to let go and then do it."

I've had to let go of so much during this journey of my life. Being a wife. My last name. My "active" status as a working mother. My privacy. My ideas about who Hank was and what we once had. These weren't things I let go of on my own time; they were snatched away, and I had no say in the matter. These things didn't abide by *Robert's Rules of Order*. They were simply painfully ripped away overnight or over time, without my permission, and certainly without my endorsement.

Now I had to give up the car that I had chosen to enrich and enable my past life. Sure, I could have bought out the lease and kept it permanently. In fact, the idea crossed my mind more than once. But there was a part of me that knew this wasn't one of the things I needed to hold on to as part of my healing—as hard as it would be, I needed to let it go. When I decided to finally do it, I sat in a parking lot and cried in fear. But I also honored my feelings. I set a boundary and rescheduled the end of my lease for the next day. I shared my brokenness with friends who loved me.

The next day—when I went to drop off the car again—was still heartbreaking, but it also felt a little different. I was letting go not by my own design, but still on my terms. I was doing it in a way that honored what holding on meant to me. I had needed to give myself time to let go of the car and all of the places I had planned to go with it. It was a small but important victory in the ability to walk away when the time was right.

Too many people focus on the *how* of letting go. We ask questions like *Was I weak? Did I cave? Did I get a vote? Was I fearful or mournful?* I have found that more important than the *how* is the *why*. Why? I was in a bad relationship. Why? Because that weight or addiction did not serve or honor me. Why? Because my world had been changed in ways I could have never imagined, yet I had to somehow move forward.

You may never understand the "how" of what happened. I surely won't. Had you been aware, could you have controlled it? If you had known, could you have done something differently? If only you could talk to that person again, could they somehow explain it? The realization that the answer to these questions is always *no* is the beginning of the letting-go process.

There are many days—then and now—when I have to look into either a physical mirror or the mirror of my heart and say, "Yes, it happened. No, it will never add up. It will never make sense. No explanation will ever quench the thirst of trauma and grief left behind." Doing this allows me to embrace what I *can* own. I can own my reactions. I can own my boundaries. I can own speaking my truth in defiant faith even when the words escaping my lips still seem hard to imagine.

On that cloudy March day in 2018 when I delivered Shimmer to the dealership, I embraced this truth. I had to both voluntarily and involuntarily walk away from all of my ideas and most of the material trappings of my former life. I had to trust that letting go might mean making space for new things. Certainly never anything or anyone to replace my daughter. But I could take back the narrative. I could add that powerful *yet* in the middle of my *before* and *after* and own what it looked like. So I turned in my safe and conservative sedan. I let go of one more physical thing that Gabrielle had touched. But I also owned the decision of what my *yet* car would look like. In this case? A bad-ass two-door sports car. A car tricked out with a sport kit that looked strikingly similar to the now-iconic one an infamous Wakandan king had dueled from in *Black Panther*. And both literally and figuratively that is what this car was. My superhero machine. My rebel hope warrior declaration for the world to keep looking. To watch me. To wonder what or who was behind the wheel. It was my way of embracing my unasked-for singleness, using it as a weapon of hope for a future I couldn't see.

I often laughed to myself when young valets at parking garages, or older suburbanites waiting for their soccer team–sized SUVs, looked longingly at my car when it pulled up. Yes, I am a woman. Yes, it is my sports car. In fact, yes, I've had a midlife crisis, although trust me, it looked nothing like yours. Yes, my life now has space for the frivolity that my newly single and childless statuses brought. No, you can't imagine it—neither can I. And yet, I am still here. I am revving up that engine and holding on tight to tomorrow as I let go of today.

You may not have the choice to own the time or place or person or thing you must let go. But that doesn't mean you have no choices left. You can still own what letting go looks like. For starters, you can let go of caring what other people may think. Nobody fully knows what it's like to live inside of your story, so nobody can tell you the full dimensions of what will help you through. You can let go of trying to please others. Your journey is about tuning in to what your mind and heart are asking for in their own quiet ways. You can let go of always putting up a brave face. We can't heal if we don't allow ourselves to grieve. You can let go of the idea of controlling anything and still hold on to everything that makes you *you*.

Let go of what you must, and also give yourself permission to hold on to what you still have. Be brave enough to acknowledge the empty spaces, but also have the courage to see the possibility of finding something else. Not something better. Not a replacement. Just something else. Sometimes you can't continue on your journey until the map flies out of the window. Hold on and let go. Surrender to the unknown journey and the unpredictable breeze. And if you're like me, harness your inner superhero and whisper under your breath, *"Wakanda Forever."*

YET

—13—

Dare to Turn the Page

April 18, 2018
A critical part of the human experience is the ability to testify
and share and bear witness to life and what you've seen. I've lost
a lot of that.

When I think about Gabrielle as a baby . . . when I want to
remember . . . I think about her father, her grandmother, and
Shelby, Gabrielle's beloved first caregiver. I am now left with
Shelby.

Shelby, a beautiful young woman who was a confident
and adventurous college student when I met her. Shelby, whose
mood and mode I gauged by her hair and nail color . . . always
wondering if the normal distractions of a young woman
in her twenties would somehow impact my baby. They
didn't.

Shelby, my only remaining source. My only remaining
connection to little phrases and words. First bumps and kisses to
make it better. First solid foods. First tastes of ice cream.

There are moments when it feels like perhaps this was all a
dream. That perhaps I never had that life. Maybe I dreamt it all
up and I've always really been alone. That the little girl I still feel
in my heart and womb was a mere figment of my imagination.
But Shelby is my confirmation that there was a time when I had
a family, a real family, with a mommy and a daddy and a little

girl with a great sense of humor, and a big smile, who was deftly,
quickly, and smartly learning the world.

As a writer, I often think about the parts of our lives in terms of a traditional story that you might learn about in English class. There are beginnings, middles, and ends. Protagonists set off on a journey, with an intention, and within a finite number of pages, they land in a world that either has given them the ending they desired or the one they needed. In the stories of life, we make the assumption that things will go the way of the Disney stories we read as a child, or even like the more sophisticated fiction we may read as adults. I once made a life out of a fairy-tale story with a man, and that story had, at its heart, a darkness I never could have dreamed of in my worst nightmares. We dare to expect continuity. If the woman had a yellow dress and couldn't dance in chapter two, we demand to know how she has come to don a red leotard and do pirouettes in chapter five. Where was the journey? The challenge with this is that there isn't just *before* and *after* like there are with many of our favorite characters. There isn't one major conflict and then an ending. There certainly can be continuity in our lives if we are willing to accept that there is the potential for many major conflicts and the likelihood that we will have to navigate this vast unknown space called *yet*.

I think that the power of story and testimony is what drew me to the book of Job in the first place. He lost more than most of us could ever imagine, and while he struggled with it, he still held on. He still had that defiant faith. You can hear the anguish in his words; they remind me of words and sentiments I expressed in my own journal entries: "Why did I not perish at birth, and die as I came from the womb? Why were there knees to receive me and breasts that I might be nursed? For now I would be lying down in peace; I would be asleep and at rest." (Job 3:11–13)

My first thoughts upon learning about Gabrielle's murder were to repeat Job's statement over and over to myself. I even remember checking my Bible on my phone as I was being driven back to my rental house from the murder scene. I needed to get it right. I'm sure I did not understand the full significance of it. There was no on-the-spot biblical exegesis happening. It just felt as though that verse would be my only connection to oxygen.

Though he slay me, yet will I trust him.

Yet will I trust him.

Yet will I trust him.

The Bible is filled with flawed men and women who are used in extraordinary ways, in spite of their ordinary talents or frailties. When I think about what it has taken for me to keep moving, there is not a singular point of inspiration. Sure, the battle and questioning of God by Job is one reference. But so is slavery in America. So are the stories of my father and mother confronting a racism that looked different than the racism we face today. I draw energy from the many stories I've covered as a journalist where I've been on the other side of the tragedy and have been inspired by how far humans can stretch themselves beyond their intellect and imaginations when called upon to do so.

Through these metaphorical holes in my body, God is shining light. It isn't the career successes or the choices I have proactively made to build my life that have wound up being my witness. It is the results of the exploded mass. It is the messy and broken bits. It is the gaping spaces that were carefully constructed and filled but now whistle with hollow isolation. But in the place of my plans, in place of my presentation, in place of the life I imagined and the self I imagined, is the absence. That is where the vulnerability is. That is what gives space for new light and new discovery to shine through. There were people who said things like "I had not prayed in ten years until Gabrielle's service" or "I lost my way with God, and watching you confirms that there must be a God." For them, I have to show up *okay*. I have accepted that as my ministry, as part of my journey.

Whenever people ask me how I do it, I say, "Well, there has to be a God or I wouldn't be alive." That's my gospel right there: I wouldn't be here without being tethered to something bigger and greater than I am. One day early on a good friend called me a supernova, and I pushed back a little. I didn't want to be super-anything. Who really wants to be in that position? Who wants to be out in the galaxy and observed from afar for some perceived courage or resilience? Who would choose to be admired for a brightness and strength that could only evolve from faith, when every bit of their mass has been blown to bits? I sure didn't. And that perspective fed into so much of what I'd experienced as a kid who felt different or like an outsider much of the time. I was the kid who was a year ahead of her age group in school. The geeky kid who was the tallest in the class. The Black kid in all-white classrooms. Feeling different wasn't new. Having people look to me as some kind of standard bearer wasn't new. Not liking that feeling wasn't new either.

Getting married and having a child were singular moments in time when I felt a very clear connection with other people. There is a universal reality, especially with children, that affords you a common dialogue. In fact, I felt most included when I was pregnant, because all of the sudden people who probably had other things in common with me but were afraid to find out considered me approachable. So this idea that I'm superhuman doesn't sit right. I'm on earth with everybody else. I don't have any special secrets or gifts to surviving tragedy, but I am willing to share what I have learned. I don't wear a cape attached to my back even when it looks like I do. The simple truth is that, for inexplicable reasons, this is my lot. So day by day and step by step I just choose to keep walking. That is what strength and resilience are all about. The choices we make, even when we wish we had other options to choose from. A choice to try. To breathe. To move. To help someone else. To love. Move by move and moment by moment, if we keep choosing to try, we will eventually find we have built something from the ashes.

If I ever concede to the idea of being a supernova, it is because of how God is using me. It is because I can clearly see how step by step my path was ordered over the years and somehow equipped me for a moment of horror that is still unimaginable. Because of this lot of mine, I learned to embrace my vulnerabilities and allowed my journey, my village, and my faith to bolster me with a confidence in a God and a faith that could even scale the unfathomable mountains I must climb. So, if I am a supernova, if watching the cataclysmic explosion of my life and body has somehow caused a warm light to fall where there was formerly darkness, and glints of warmth from mass deconstructed somehow give you the courage to look directly into the blinding brightness for your *yet*, then use me and step into your own unique light.

Resilience is absolutely about embracing your vulnerability. As much as I don't like the supernova or superhero persona, nobody wants to be seen blown to bits or crumpled in a corner in the dark either. And yet, sometimes that is what the grieving process looks like. We must show vulnerability, not because we are brave, but because we have no other options. We must ask for help because we have no other choice. In moments of weakness and despair, something miraculous happens. Through your weakness and need, God shows up for you through someone else. Through someone who may find out in *your* moment that *they* have strength they were unaware of too.

Perhaps one of the most isolating things about grief is the unexpected moments. Sure, on anniversaries, birthdays, and holidays, I anticipate reflecting and mourning. I expect to feel the depth of my loss then. People who love me always gather around me to ensure I'm not alone on those days. But it's the moments that are completely unexpected that can knock me off my feet. Moments like watching my fellow Howard University sorority sister Kamala Harris become the vice president-elect of the United States of America. With all of the joy and excitement, the surreal nature of the moment, all I could think about was Gabrielle. I cried because I remembered Gabrielle's curiosity about my sorority, Alpha Kappa Alpha, and my sorority sisters—Black women with every type of career possible, breaking glass ceilings in pink heels every day. She bounced in her stroller at the center of our circle as we sang our songs at Howard's homecoming.

Any celebratory feelings for the new vice president were overwhelmed by my sorrow. As social media lit up with mothers and daughters who recognized themselves in Kamala Harris and her story, I felt the isolating grief of no longer finding myself there. No longer a wife. No longer a mother. No longer holding the small hand of a little girl in a pretty dress and pigtails.

Grief doesn't allow for a forecast or even a mood ring to warn me of these moments. So when they come so unexpectedly, I have to fight the temptation to hide. Instead, I write or testify or seek comfort in those who love me. It is not easy to do in these "pop-up" moments, but I know that the only way I can truly take care of myself is if I can learn to push myself out of the isolation and allow space and air for a loved one to stand in the pain with me.

When we consciously present as strong, our actions are sometimes interpreted to mean that we are resistant to being vulnerable. That's not the case for me. Brené Brown, author of *The Gifts of Imperfection* and *Daring Greatly*, said, "Vulnerability is . . . having the courage to show up and be seen when we have no control over the outcome. Vulnerability is not weakness; it's our greatest measure of courage."

Maybe it is the storyteller in me. My story isn't about *how* I show up. Full face or not. Strong countenance or in tears. My story is about the fact that I show up in spite of what happened to me. I am an expressive person, so in addition to the responsibility I feel to let everyone know I'm okay, I'm also acutely aware of my need to connect my experiences to people who love me.

As with all of us, the pivotal experiences of my life have weaved together the sometimes beautiful, sometimes faded and frayed threads that make up the tapestry of my personal story. That tapestry shows people how I operate in the world.

My mother used to say, "the only thing constant is change." Being the child who hated change, that would frustrate me. I cried at the end of the school year and at the beginning too. I cried when I was dropped off at college and cried when my parents came to pick me up after that first year. New things were frightening to me. That's why it's so amazing—and slightly ironic—that God would use *me* to testify about anything. The little girl who hid in her mother's skirt? The little girl who ran to the back of the school bus to wave at her mother while her mom followed the bus to school? The little girl who scared easily and cried as a baby whenever her picture was taken? The one who crept into her parents' bedroom at night to make sure her mother was still breathing? The young woman who still called home after she'd left to start her own

life to make sure her mom was there? And when my mother was no longer there, I was propelled into my becoming. I had to draw on all of the
scripts and all of the rehearsals of my previous life. I had to unearth all
the things that had somehow become rote theory and become unflap-
pable in my defiant faith.

— 14 —

Seek Inspiration

Every month, on the first Sunday, my church sings the hymn "It Is Well with My Soul" after Communion.

When peace like a river attendeth my way
When sorrows like sea billows roll
Whatever my lot, Thou hast taught me to say
It is well, it is well with my soul
It is well
With my soul
It is well, it is well with my soul

I do believe that sometimes our spirits will foreshadow a future event in our lives that we can't see until we get there. Every month, when we'd sing this song, I'd cry. At the time, I didn't know why it moved me so. But when Gabrielle died, "It Is Well" was the only song I requested for the service.

The author of the lyrics, Horatio G. Spafford, lost his four remaining children (he'd already lost a child to scarlet fever) when the ship they were on from America to England sank. On his own voyage to England, to meet up with his wife, who was the sole family survivor of the tragedy, the captain notified him when they were passing over the spot in the sea where the accident happened. At that moment in the journey, these lyrics came to him. According to the historical record, "words of comfort and hope" filled this man as the ship sailed smoothly over the watery grave of his beloved children.

Spafford's words and story give me strength because they remind me that I am not alone on this journey; that those who have walked this path before me have left me help along their way. Those lyrics remind me that it is possible to embrace hope no matter what; to stand in a faith that holds everything externally together, even when everything inside feels broken. Those words gave me the nerve to stand at my baby's funeral, in front of thousands of people, dressed in white, shoulders and back straight, declaring to everyone, including the devil himself, that I would not be moved. Grief was surely present, but so was the faith that sealed me up in an armor of fortitude that day. With each wobbly step, I had hope that Gabrielle's legacy would live on. It was that hope, that faith, that afforded me the strength to be the one to close her casket. I was the first person she touched in this world, and I was going to be the last one to touch the shell where her spirit had been held.

Faith was not my only armor that day, though, or any of the days I have spent moving out of my *before*. I have borrowed strength, inspiration, fortitude, and courage from all manner of places. A few months before I lost Gabrielle, I read the book *The Underground Railroad* by Colson Whitehead. I was immediately drawn to the story because the main character's name was Cora, and my beloved mother's name was Cora. Reading it took me to a place in my body that felt like I was experiencing the grief and terror from past generations that I had not personally ever known. It was the story of slavery in America with all of its brutal cruelty and of a reimagined version of the Underground Railroad, the network that helped some slaves escape to the North before emancipation. As an African American, there's something about imagining what our ancestors endured during the transatlantic slave trade that rumbles the deepest part of me. They were the progenitors of the defiant faith we claim today. How dare we not make it? How dare we not make sure little Black girls and boys who come after us have something that we didn't have? This reminder of where I come from drives me. How dare I turn my back on everything that's gotten me where I am today? Yes, I could cry out, "why me?" But then, "why anyone?" No one should *have* to endure this. And yet, because I stand on the shoulders of generations of people who were unjustly persecuted, killed, and whose families were destroyed, I know that the defiant will to survive is in my DNA and makes me strong.

Another piece of the puzzle for me was understanding the science of how we experience and process extreme and pervasive pain. Bessel van der Kolk, in his book *The Body Keeps the Score*, talks quite a bit about the ways trauma can show up in our physical bodies.

> *As human beings we belong to an extremely resilient species . . . but traumatic experiences do leave traces, whether on a large scale (on our histories and cultures) or close to home, on our families, with dark secrets being imperceptibly passed down through generations. They also leave traces on our minds and emotions, on our capacity for joy and intimacy, and on our biology and immune systems. . . .*
>
> *Trauma compromises the brain area that communicates the physical, embodied feeling of being alive.*

This was very true for me right after Gabrielle's murder and in the days and months leading up to the trial. I would often find myself sick, as if my body was giving out. I felt weak and depleted. My sleep was disrupted with nightmares. If I slept more than four hours—forget consecutively—it was a victory. The first question loved ones would ask when I talked to them was "How did you sleep last night?"

When I was still long enough, the emptiness would settle in. Even when I pushed myself hard and ran a hundred miles per hour through my days, I'd still wind up restless and overwhelmed at the end of it all. I wanted someone to help me, but I also knew I could only save myself.

It took time for me to realize that these feelings weren't about my faith or God. They weren't an indication of my tolerance for justice or a measure of my strength. It was simply the process my body and mind needed to go through to heal. It was and is the impossible step-by-step and breath-by-breath process I alone am responsible for enduring. No one knows brokenness and betrayal better than I do. I'm aware of both

God's strength and my own weakness. But my humanity matters also. The woman in me struggles and needs inspiration to keep going. The mother in me sometimes can't understand how to go on. I know that time moves on. Children who were once seven years old with Gabrielle are growing up. And I have made peace with the duality of celebrating the hallmarks of their lives and yet grieving for my own baby. I have created my own playbook and occasionally thrown out my own rules to begin again.

I have learned that courage and strength and healing come in a million different forms. Laughing at a mindless comedy with friends. Going out to dinner. Taking a walk for air when you want nothing but to hide under the covers. Asking for help donating baby clothes that you had imagined would someday be handed down to younger siblings. Some of my efforts to seek inspiration have required me to find it first within myself. I have learned to prop myself up. I have learned to look in the mirror at the end of a hard day and smile at myself. I have learned to repeat out loud words of inspiration that hung on closet doors and bathroom mirrors in my home.

People tell me to my face and whisper as I walk away that they don't know how I do it. Maybe you know what it feels like to watch people's expressions change, their conversations stop, their voices alter when you come near. Maybe you see heads lean together to whisper when you walk away. When they say, "I don't know how you do it," sometimes I want to tell them, "I don't do it." When I need to, I send a hollow version of my former self into the world to represent something still, solid, and hopeful. Not everybody needs to see the wide range of emotions I cycle through. And that's okay. That separation allows me the space to heal. To do what's necessary for my soul, while still inspiring others on their grief journeys.

The truth is, we're all made differently. The way each of us holds our pain and promise differs from person to person. To say that one type of painting is more beautiful than another, or one type of bird or flower is better than another, is to speak about preference and not fact. We are all created to be who we are, and we will express our emotions and create our survival plans differently. It is not about expressing grief and pain the way I express mine because, by the way, when the door shuts, I fall apart just like anyone else.

I think one of the gifts, as strange as it sounds, of losing my mother and grandmother at twenty-four is I learned early on that people grieve differently. It is important to be gracious in your grief and with your healing. If grace and self-compassion mean having your house filled with reminders of your *before*, so be it. If it means covering or burning every picture, then that's okay too. You can take advice from a doctor, pastor, or therapist, yes. You can even listen to a person who has written a book about going through something similar—or going through something very different, but with a framework for survival that resonates with you. But finding the things that bring you peace and inspiration will be very personal and specific to your journey.

One of the ways I've been able to seek inspiration is through meditation. It isn't a strength of mine at all. I struggle with raging thoughts. But I've found in these last few years that anything that allows me to go inward—to calm my nervous system when the waves of grief and trauma hit—is comforting. Focusing on my breath in moments of panic or trauma is everything.

I wish I had a single answer to those who want to know the best ways to "go inward." I have always prayed, and yes, there are times when prayers seem rote or ritual at best. Sometimes my prayers just look like me crying in the corner. I have done some meditation. Breathing exercises, similar to those I learned for Lamaze class while practicing for natural childbirth, are a really great way to bring the heart rate down and calm the mind when I feel panicked. The inhale and exhale gave me a laser-like focus and steadied me in the face of pain. These breathing exercises came in handy in the medical examiner's office while viewing Gabrielle's body. They were the same exercises I practiced while walking into the funeral parlor. They steadied me walking into the courtroom to sit and bear witness to the story.

I also think communing with nature, or building a ritual around the outdoors, can be an important source of comfort. Whether it is a hiking trail, a snowy slope, or a sandy beach that helps you get outside yourself—literally and figuratively—find inspiration in nature and the natural beauty that surrounds you. You may find that you already have consistent ways to get an infusion of inspiration—a particular song, motivational speech, sermon, or mantra you say over and over. Having your go-to methods is vital when things get hectic. You have to be open to those spontaneous signs and not miss the moments. Inspiration and affirmation from the universe that you are on the right track may come in a loving text or email, a beautiful songbird outside of your window, or the paradox of dark clouds full of rain sharing space with a rainbow. These various forms of inspiration are an integral part of the supplies we need for our journey. They give us emotional strength and food for our soul. Be clear about what inspires and motivates you. Make space for the rigor of self-care in the same way you make time and space for those you love. Having these tools at the ready ensures you can access your strength to take the reins when you can and summon the peace to let go when you must.

— 15 —

Keep Getting Up

Gabrielle was a part of Girl Scout Troop 2988. She'd gone from being a Daisy to going through the bridging ceremony where she became a Brownie. Every time I look at her Brownie sash and all the patches she earned, I'm reminded of how this crazy working mom wanted to iron on the patches and her grandmother would lovingly sew them each on to make sure they stayed. And cookie season? Whew! Selling Girl Scout cookies was not for the faint of heart. It was truly hardcore. Because I was a Girl Scout myself only for a brief time, I didn't really understand what I was embarking on when I volunteered to be one of the cookie moms. Nevertheless, I knew how much it meant to Gabrielle for me to be involved, and I wanted her to earn the cool patch she'd get as a result. She loved rubbing her hand across that "cookie mom" patch and remembering how hard we worked.

So I decided that I wanted to start creating opportunities and exposure for the things that meant everything to Gabrielle. In our town of New Rochelle, there was a Girl Scout community house that all of the Girl Scouts in the county used for various events. It's a beautiful old house where members hold meetings, learn to cook, and do bridging ceremonies. Because of the age of the home, the kitchen looked like something from the *Brady Bunch* era. Gabrielle and I loved to cook so much. It was such an intimate activity that we shared. Every weekend, from the time she was big enough to get on a chair and stand next to me at the counter, we baked or cooked. The kitchen was where we pretended to be on the Food Network as she beckoned her grandmother, papa, or anyone else who was around to serve as our audience and watch what we were doing. So when I thought about where to start in terms of donations, starting close to home meant starting close to Gabrielle's heart. Because she loved baking and she loved the Girl Scouts, the idea of updating and renovating the kitchen felt like a wonderful way to get started.

I purposely chose Gabrielle's eighth birthday because, though she wouldn't be with me, I could be with her friends and feel close to her in a very communal way. I think this might have been the live news television producer in me, always looking down the road to plan and mitigate things that can be seen from a distance. As part of my survival tactics, I planned out each potential "trigger" day or anniversary with a way to make it as bearable as possible. I was deliberate and methodical about how I would approach this day. I had to be. It was the way I survived each day and forced myself to get out of bed. I chose that day because I didn't want to be alive, but giving my first donation in her name would give me somewhere I was obligated to be instead of sinking in the comfort of pure darkness. I needed a responsibility I couldn't shirk regardless of how I felt.

On that day, several of my friends met at the house in advance. My "army" had arrived. They are jokingly called "the 300," a nickname that came from the story of the three hundred Persian soldiers who were matched against an army of three hundred thousand and somehow still prevailed. My life and my story have felt that way. The insurmountable war of evil included legal red tape, financial distress, broken hearts and spirits, and sheer terror. And my "300" is standing with me ready to push forward and fight like hell. I am grateful for everyone who stands in the corner waiting to try to catch me when I fall. I'm grateful for everyone who walks behind me desperate to be given instructions on something tangible they can do; to somehow demonstrate that they are here for me.

When they arrived, they were somber and anxious, mostly because they were not sure how I would feel. Everyone wore a Gabrielle button, and we drove together in a caravan to the Girl Scout house. The small event included the mayor and a city councilman, the Girl Scout troops from around the area, and their moms.

I painfully remember walking into the house that day. My dad had slept at my house the night before. There was nothing that was said that day by me or anyone else that could speak as loud as what was unsaid: I was walking into a room full of little girls in brown sashes who missed their friend. Little girls who couldn't understand what happened. Who were less than sixty days out from what was probably the most traumatic experience they'd ever had. Who typically spent the August 2 weekend enjoying the crazy TV producer–level parties I threw for my baby every year. But now they were standing in a room acknowledging their friend as an angel whose earthly growth had stopped, while they continued to move on. All eyes were on me, the mom who'd made up the cheer that we drowned out the other troops with at the Thanksgiving parade and who was now with them to pay tribute to her child's birthday and short life. The heartbreak and hope of Gabrielle's fellow troop members and their parents was evident. The support for me was palpable. Especially from moms and daughters who clutched each other as they approached me nervously for a hug.

I think what was most important in that first year about these types of events was that they gave me something to focus on. I had to get dressed. I had to prepare words to say. I had to somehow convey to the mothers and children who were there with tearstained faces that I would make it. And because I would make it, they would make it too. I became an extremely reluctant symbol of fortitude and resilience. No matter how much I didn't want to be those things, I knew it was important to the people who were around me. Sometimes in our efforts to stand tall and keep moving for others, we are actually creating our own healing. In our attempt to help ease the walk of those around us, we can find ourselves just a few steps farther down the road.

— 16 —

Control What You Can

In production, we sometimes joke that the actual performances or live events are the easy part. At that point, the lights are on and all you can do is take the ride. You're not really in control anymore. All you can do is be present and have faith that the pre-production prep you did left you ready for the unknown. Sometimes that's all that matters, friend. As Donnie McClurkin's powerful gospel song, "Stand," instructs: *What do you do when you've done all you can? . . . Well you just stand when there's nothing left to do/You just stand, watch the Lord see you through/Yes, after you've done all you can/You just stand.*

In the early days afterward, I began to create rituals to help me find my footing and anchor me in the new world. Things I could do with repetition that would remind me to keep breathing. To keep going. It's devastating to realize just how little control we have. Over and over again, like Job, "though he slay me yet will I trust him" was my battle cry. I would search and search the remaining chapters in the Book of Job for answers. Grappling with the unknown was painful but useful. It taught me that resilience is built, question after question, from the inside out.

Life sometimes requires you to prepare for battle. The battle can be internal. Or the battle can literally play out in a courtroom theater, around a company conference table, or in a couple's bedroom. As you prepare to face difficult conversations or traumatic events, think of yourself as an athlete. Visualize how you want to show up—literally and figuratively. That may even involve talking to yourself in the mirror as you plot out a conversation. Listen to your body. Like an athlete, what do you need to give yourself in self-care and self-awareness to ensure your emotional health and safety? How can you play out various unknown scenarios, perhaps even with a friend or confidant? Athletes practice. They prepare for various weather conditions. They know their competition. They make sure they have the proper equipment. They visualize crossing the finish line victoriously. In some ways, you can too. Own your power and take control of the elements of your circumstances that you do have control over.

And as you do that work, give yourself the gift of vulnerability. It may not feel like a gift, especially if it is unusual or unfamiliar for you. However, part of controlling what you can is outsourcing. It is bringing in "experts" to tackle things that perhaps you could, but don't need to expend the emotional energy for. It can be as complex as legal or medical advice or as simple but lifesaving as planning meals or carpooling. You will find that sharing the weight of the load you carry is not just helpful to you, but that vulnerability allows for the gift of intimacy with those who choose to walk by your side and carry for you what they can.

After the initial criminal investigation, it was years before my legal challenges even began to subside. I was forced to deal with juggling a series of legal storms all at once. A divorce that my husband was somehow fighting from behind bars. A house that had become a crime scene that I could not stomach to enter again in foreclosure, with ongoing legal threats from banks and the homeowners association. And, of course, the unknown fear and anxiety around the criminal trial. The trial ironically started around the second anniversary of Gabrielle's murder. There were delays after delays. When the proceedings finally started, I wasn't allowed in the courtroom until after I testified.

After anticipating the trial for so long, it felt almost like an out-of-body experience. I had friends who were former prosecutors and helped prepare me. I had other friends who worked as journalists and joined me in the briefings with the DA. One of my close friends, Desi, was friends with a professional stylist who'd worked on *Law & Order*; she helped me pick out things that would tell the jury who I was in a way that would be palatable. Plain solid pieces in dark colors. A simple pearl necklace and earrings. Knee-length dresses and skirts instead of pants. All of that sounds ridiculous now, but it meant everything to me at the time to feel as though I had chosen the armor that could protect me from what was coming.

Because of my role in the trial, I was not able to be there every day. My community organized what would typically be a meal train but instead became a courtroom sitting train. People who loved me and loved Gabrielle could sign up to participate by sitting in the courtroom every day. There were also some people who had never even met Gabrielle but who were willing to take a time slot and bear witness. When I think about what they endured, seeing what I couldn't see, it astounds me. The courtroom was packed every day. People flew in from all over the country. The Five, short for "five the hard way" as they are listed in my phone, is the name I gave five of my closest friends. They were in full effect, 24/7. My friend Tara took a short leave of absence from work in Seattle to be with me. There were actual meal trains as well, to make sure that those who would convene back at the house after the day in court would have food.

Everything about court is fluid. As concrete as the law is, there is more gray area than we typically think when it comes to details. The trial date kept being moved. Initially, I was told to anticipate it being about a hundred days after my daughter's murder. But, a hundred days turned into two years. I was told that because of the time of year, the July 4 holiday would somehow fall during the trial, and that because the judge had already taken a week off for vacation, there would literally be a vacation week during it. It is a surreal thing to have everything in your world hang on the choices and convenience of others. Suddenly your destiny and peace of mind are determined by fitting into a calendar shaped by the mundanity of other people's schedules; what for you is a life-altering event can be, for many other people involved, simply a day job. For them, it was about getting their job done along with whatever personal things they needed to do. We were simply another thing on the grid.

Starting with the stifling conference room where I was first ushered into the Special Prosecutions Division of Westchester County and the only female ADA present said on day one, "What did you do to make him hate you so much?" It felt like a surreal dream of darkness. I was cloaked in secrecy as cameras waited out front to try to get a shot of me—the victim of the latest crime scandal. There were amazing public servants—and some not so amazing—I met as I navigated the ups and downs of logistical and legal red tape before finally getting to the trial. Despite the blessing of many expert personal resources and a journalism background, it was often an intimidating and confusing process.

My father somehow found the steel in his veins to be at the trial every day. I begged him not to sit through the medical examiner's report, because as a reporter, I had done that and I knew what it entailed. But no, he was there. It was like he'd taken on the role of host, introducing himself and giving summaries to friends, family, church members, and coworkers about where things stood. To this day, people talk to me about how much of a rock he was during the trial. I know my father wishes he could turn back the clock and somehow anticipate Hank's evil plot so that none of this ever happened, so maybe that was part of the reason why he remained steadfast and unmoved during the grueling nightmare that unfolded. He was going to stand up for his daughter and granddaughter in any way he could.

I wasn't allowed into the courtroom until after I'd testified, which didn't happen for a few days. Family and friends would share what they could without jeopardizing my testimony. It was frustrating to be in the dark, so I'd take in everything they said carefully because I wanted to be prepared for any and every scenario. The writer and journalist in me had nearly as many questions for the district attorneys as they had for me.

I wanted to ensure that I was doing everything possible to stand up for my Gabi Bear the best way I could, so, in my mind, I needed to remember everything. I carried around a small black notebook I'd started carrying after I asked Hank for a divorce. The early pages were scribbles of potential attorneys, fees, and information about things like child support and equitable distribution. Several pages in, it became a completely different book. In hindsight, I can see my duality clearly in those pages. There was a trained journalist covering a murder trial, who needed all the details, and a mother who was desperate to do everything in her power to push for whatever flimsy earthly justice was possible for Gabrielle's murderer. I would wake up in the middle of the night and remember a conversation with Hank or find an email or see a text and want to forward it immediately to the DA. There could be no stone left unturned.

I had no idea what to expect, but I prepared to engage in a war with faceless threats and unknown enemy "incoming." I journaled about important details. I created a whole folder in my email of things I wanted to ensure I remembered to bring up, if relevant, during the trial. I would wake up in the middle of the night or pull over while driving when a thought came to mind. My short-term memory had been severely disrupted by the trauma of Gabrielle's murder, so I was always fearful of forgetting something important. My subject-less emails to myself, my scribblings in my journal or voice notes in my phone, were a frenetic battle plan that could be organized and inserted where needed. During my matrimony court appearances as I fought to be granted a divorce from a murderer. As I passionately wrote my victim impact statement during the sentencing. I didn't know what was coming or what to expect, so I controlled what I could. I was informed. I was prepared. I tried to take care of myself physically.

Another way I had prepared for the trial was by creating what I called my "court playlist" long in advance. It was a complete mashup of who I was. Moving gospel songs that reminded me of my childhood and hardcore gangster rap that said I wasn't to be messed with. Before going into court and facing the jury one day, I sat in the car with my freshman-year college roommate Karla, a pediatrician who knew and loved Gabrielle, me, and hip-hop. In our church/court clothes, we blasted Public Enemy and Ice Cube and sang all the words at the top of our lungs like teenagers while parked across the street from the courthouse. As I walked out of the courtroom later that day, after testifying, Public Enemy was playing somewhere in the ether. When Hank's defense attorney questioned my memory and my loyalty to my daughter, I gave myself permission to let that rage and audacity fuel my determination to stay strong and do what I needed to do for Gabrielle and myself. Life sometimes requires us to develop muscles we didn't know we even had. We wake up sore realizing our bodies have been tasked with something new. Just like you would mentally and physically prepare for a marathon, situations that hold trauma, pain, grief, or fear may require new physical and emotional routines. Some of the things I did were tactical, some were planned, some were suggested by friends or my therapist. But I was open to my vulnerability and was able to say, "I don't know what this is. I have never been here before. This race looks infinite. What tools do I need? What advice do I need? What tangible and intangible exercises must I master in order to face my unknown?"

If you've ever started a workout routine, you've probably heard about or used resistance training. Resistance training increases our muscle strength by making our muscles work against a pressure or weight. To truly gain benefits, you have to achieve the "progressive overload principle." That means you have to do strength-training activities to the point where it is hard for you to do another repetition. You have to push and challenge yourself. Without that resistance, your body will not achieve its full resilience.

I've come to believe that our emotional resilience follows a similar philosophy. Resilience is a muscle. We build it in the same ways we build our bodies. We can feed it through prayer, meditation, or journaling. We starve it with negativity and surrounding ourselves with those who drain our energy reserves. Resilience also requires you to hold on to hope at all costs. Yes, you will feel the tension between hope and helplessness; that's part of the journey. But as a warrior, you can always make the choice to hope.

We don't get stronger by harnessing the speeding trajectory of a life moving in the direction we desire. We develop our resilience muscles through resistance. From our childhood days on soccer and softball fields, we might have learned that how we lose is at least as important as how we win. Many career professionals will tell you that the last two weeks of a job are just as important as the first two.

Sometimes in resistance training you can literally feel your muscles spasm and shake. It feels like one more rep could be the one where your arms fall off your body like a *Looney Tunes* character. If you are working with a trainer, you may give them death stares because it seems like they are literally trying to break you. Then it happens. You push through. You let go of the fear of the outcome and focus solely on trying. You let go of all your expectations and harness all of that energy to fight against the tremendous weight at (or in!) hand.

The same is true with emotional resilience. You can build your emotional muscles when they are challenged, even to the breaking point. Resilience doesn't mean winning. It means not giving up. Resilience doesn't guarantee answers, but it does give you the strength to let go of your expectations of the inexplicable.

Resilience for me has looked like showing up to speak at Gabrielle's funeral. It has also looked like bowing out of dinner plans with a friend when it feels like I am going to crumble. Perhaps one of the toughest moments of resilience was during the criminal trial. After three different criminal defense attorneys for Hank and numerous court delays, the trial finally began. My TV remained dark and I relied solely on friends, family, and the DA for updates instead of the news. Then the day came. I was expected to testify. I had spent months and years anticipating that moment. With my therapist, Caroline, I forced myself to listen to Hank's voice and see his image on news stories from his arrest and indictment. On the day I was supposed to testify, I was holed up in a small and stifling conference room with my childhood best friend, Tara. It was windowless and warm. I was wearing my "uniform" as prescribed and was trying desperately not to sweat through my hair or leave stains under the arms of my dress. It was a Friday and I got updates all day letting me know how things were progressing in the courtroom. As the day grew later and later, I feared they wouldn't get to me. I feared another sleepless night and nerve-wracking weekend before I was back in that suffocating conference room with the old, motel-quality television perched high, waiting to be called into the courtroom. As the afternoon began to tick along, I became more and more nervous the closer we got to the 4 p.m. stop time. I no longer felt confident that my singular human strength could fight against the weight of expectation. Then I did it. I didn't give up, but I gave in. I let go. I had no control over what was happening in that courtroom. I could only control how I rode the waves and held up my weight. I kicked off my uncomfortable "church" shoes and started pacing and humming the gospel song "I Surrender All." As I look back, I can only imagine what I must have looked like. Crazy? Maybe. But also determined even in the midst of sorrow and fear. Surrendered? Definitely. I surrendered to my faith, knowing that sometimes just letting go of a particular outcome is victory enough. Thirty minutes before the court adjourned for the day, I got the call.

I wouldn't have time to fully testify or be cross-examined before the weekend, but they were going to get me on the stand. If nothing else, I would see him. I would identify him. As I walked into the courtroom, I continued to let go of any expectations. I released how I looked or walked. I passed family and members of the 300 as I headed to the witness stand. Under my arm I gripped my purse that secretly held Barbara, while standing and raising my right hand. I sat with my back erect and touched one of the pearl stud earrings my friend Lucia had given me for this day. I vowed to tell the truth. I said my name. I identified my daughter's murderer.

Resilience isn't about what you expect or anticipate. There is no linear A to Z on grief or loss. The music continues to play. The record may skip. The song may change tempo. The choreography may momentarily compete with the melody. Whatever happens, keep dancing. Sometimes it isn't about your "moves," just your bravery to stay on the dance floor.

And much like physical resistance training, we can't predict or necessarily visualize what the fruits of our labor will look like. But if we keep standing, if we hold on while our arms are shaking and begging us to give up, if we learn the magical dance of holding on and letting go all at the same time, our faith won't fail us.

I HAVE DRAWN enormous strength from my friends, family, and community. I have drawn enormous strength from my own rituals, history, and heritage. But it is also incredibly important to note that I have drawn strength from working with professionals who have been trained to help people process the unimaginable. And that is why another important way to control what we can is through therapy. My therapist, Caroline Kern, had a background in the Manhattan DA's office. When we first started working together, I had been incredibly intentional to pick someone who got it. She was from my town. She was a mom. And she understood violent trauma. I needed more than grief counseling and she got that. Because I had experienced loss and "normal" grief counseling when my mother died decades earlier, I knew this was different. I had done stories about women with the frozen shock and emptiness that I now saw in my own eyes. A comforting bereavement specialist was not going to be enough. When we met for the first time, tears gathered in the corners of her eyes as she admitted to knowing my story. She let off a few colorful words as we talked, which, frankly, endeared her to me even more. At the end of our first meeting, I looked at her and said, "I like you. You're smart and you swear. I'll be coming back."

And I'm still coming back. There have been countless hours of texts, calls, meetings, and court appearances that she has done, yes because she's a counselor, but mostly because she is a woman and a mother. This woman trained me like a prizefighter for what lay ahead. Given her background, she knew what I was facing even though I did not. She knew the complexity and constraints of the judicial system. She knew that my trauma was so pronounced that I needed tools to pull myself back from the edge in the middle of the night. And because of her training, she had those tools, which she was able to share with me. A rubber band on my wrist to literally "snap" me back at times. A mental picture of Gabrielle lying next to me in bed to call on when the images of her after her death haunted me.

When it came time to prepare to see Hank in court, Caroline started showing me pictures of him. Then videos so I could watch him move. Then, we worked on enduring the sound of his voice. She went with me to every single court hearing. Whether it was a divorce hearing where we sat outside for several hours only to find out that he had opted out of showing up from prison, or the murder trial, or the sentencing. Caroline was always close by.

In many ways, she was my justice doula, reminding me how to

breathe. Reminding me how to move and be in and out of my body as necessary for survival throughout the process. I was releasing from my body the turmoil, hate, and pain that had been set upon me. It was going to require the same level of discipline, concentration, breathing, and focus that had been required to bring Gabrielle into the world after twenty-seven hours without anesthesia. It required planning, drills, and exercises so that my mental muscle memory would know what to do in volatile and unknown circumstances. Having Caroline in my corner—to lend me her confidence when I needed it, but also so much more—was critical.

There are moments in our lives—both good and bad—that we can anticipate and imagine. There are also the times when we are knocked completely off our feet and left literally breathless. They both require preparation. Pregnant mommies may plan for natural childbirth but might also have to be ready for an emergency C-section. Whatever the scenario, allow yourself to be coached. Allow yourself to ask for what you need and seek out "experts" who can help you along the path you can see and perhaps through the dark doorway ahead. Your ability to raise your head above roaring rapids and scream will enable someone to throw you that lifeline.

Control what you can and then just stand.

— 17 —

Speak Your Truth

I'm a fighter. I always have been. Being that way is helpful when you work in a business where you hear *no* a hundred times more than *maybe* or *yes*. There was no way I was hearing *no* when it came to honoring Gabrielle. There was no way that I was not going to do everything possible and think of every single possibility to ensure that my sweet girl was illuminated in the way that she needed to be in court. Life calls on all of us in different ways to stand and bear witness. It may not be in a courtroom, and I hope, for your sake, it isn't in a violent criminal trial. But there are times in our lives when there are onlookers who we wish weren't watching us walk naked in our testimony. Those who sit in judgment without all the information. Don't be afraid in those moments to sit or stand with your back erect, smooth out your garments, clear your voice, and speak your truth.

The district attorney's office did not think they needed to prepare me for cross-examination, so I sat in front of Hank's third court-appointed attorney—a ragged man in an ill-fitting suit rumbling through scrambled notes—waiting for whatever might come. Hank had refused to plead guilty. After confessing to the police on the scene, he sat there incredulously saying he was innocent. The defense was trying to suggest natural causes.

When my time came to speak, I sat tall and erect. Broken, but determined. I was a victim, but it was important for me to convey another image. An image that could stand against the one associated with bloody knives and rearranged stuffed animals; with a murder scene planned for hours and staged to look like something else altogether. I had enough legal professionals in my village to know that even the superficial would send signals to the jury about who I was. I needed them to focus on the heartbroken mother versus the media business executive. I knew Hank's court-appointed attorney would use everything possible to try to create suspicion in the eyes of the jury. Every decision, from my choice of earrings to my selection of shoes, had been carefully considered. I crafted a figure for every person in that courtroom to remember at night at home as they hugged their own living children.

I sat on the stand, poised, but raging on the inside, as this defense attorney cross-examined me about Gabrielle's medication.

"Didn't she have asthma?"

"Wasn't she taking a lot of medication?"

After pointing to her medical history, he turned to mine.

"Don't you have a history of migraines?"

Yes, more than a decade ago.

"Did you ever pass out when you had those migraines?"

Yes, more than a decade ago.

And then:

"Are you sure that you know where you were on June 6, 2017?"

At that point, I realized that the district attorney had been wrong. I wasn't prepared enough for how this defense attorney would use what is called the scorched-earth method to somehow discredit me. I pushed my purse holding Barbara closer to my body. I adjusted myself in the seat on the stand. My voice dropped lower and got slower and more measured. I looked straight into Hank's eyes and then back to his attorney, who was about to realize that he had summoned, as Gabrielle would have said, Mommy Monster. I laid out the realities of that day, and the circumstances leading up to it: Hank's lack of parental support or supervision that required a full-time nanny even though he was unemployed. And I questioned his defense attorney's lack of medical expertise or evidence when he tried to suggest that Gabrielle's health could have played a factor in her death. I asked if I could say anything else, and both the judge and the defense attorney simultaneously exclaimed, "No!"

I did what I'd come to do. I somehow managed to take the liquid that was my legs and create enough solids to stand up and walk off the stand. I smoothed my dress and my hair. I looked over at Hank as he looked away, and I walked out of the courtroom. That was me, controlling what I could.

Sometimes all the preparation and this notion of controlling what we can boils down to speaking your truth. And sometimes speaking your truth is less about the words that come out of your mouth and more about the conviction with which they are delivered. It's about the bravery it takes to try. Your truth might come out in muffled cries or brilliant eloquence. It might involve alliteration or expletives worthy of a pirate. Just be honest. We might not always want to be honest with others, for a whole host of reasons that are both practical and political, and frankly, pertinent to our survival. But we must be able to be honest with ourselves. In order to grow and heal, we must first get on the witness stand of our lives, raise our hand, and look in the mirror. We must be willing to tell ourselves the whole truth and nothing but the truth. Our naked honesty with ourselves and those whom we deem worthy to share with is so necessary. What happens to you, including the darkness in your life, whether it was thrown upon you or is self-inflicted, is now also a part of your story. The dark streaks or embarrassing flashes of color that you would have never intended for your life's canvas are all required for you to see and claim your *after*. Sometimes those unwanted or unexpected shadows allow for a deeper and richer picture when you take a step back. You may be surprised how the contrast and colors you dread in the picture of your story just might offer light or hope to someone else.

Whatever trials you are facing, I hope that you can get on your personal witness stand and tell your story. Tell your truth. Brace yourself and challenge yourself. Your story may not look the way you thought it would. The settings and characters may change. But it's still your story. Look in that dirty mirror and know that those are still your eyes. That is still your mouth. This is still your moment to ensure that your version of your history is unapologetically told. I thought I was doing it just for Gabrielle at the time. But now I know I was also doing it for myself.

— 18 —

Visualize All Possibilities

After two years of waiting and weeks of a painful public trial, the verdict arrived unexpectedly. We had been sent home by the DA during deliberations. The July 4 weekend was coming up and they didn't see a verdict happening anytime soon. I took off my "uniform" and tried not to fear the worst. What if they had enough doubt to let him go free? I took several out-of-town family members to see some of the things I had done through Gabrielle's Wings. The library space. The Girl Scout kitchen. As we sat in the parking lot where Gabrielle's Playground shoots up toward the sky with butterfly images, I received several frantic calls. The jury was back. The judge was ready to reconvene. I had thirty minutes to get to a courthouse thirty minutes away—in rush hour—because they wouldn't wait for my return to render the verdict. In a panic, two cars of family raced back toward the courthouse. The woman who showed up, with her T-shirt and shorts, her flip-flops and scattered hair, tightly grasping a doll that had been the first security blanket for her murdered baby, did not have time for perfection. There was no way to fashionably or coolly mask the panic I felt when I thought I might not arrive in time to be in the room when the ruling was read. I raced through the courthouse entrance and screamed into the phone for the DA's office to send someone to park my car. There was a crowd waiting outside. Someone from the DA's office rushed us up the stairs, no time for an elevator. We burst in and disrupted the silence of the courtroom. The judge looked up as if I was clearly keeping him from starting his July 4 holiday weekend. He asked for the jury to be brought back into the courtroom. I tried to imagine what would happen as I attempted to meet eyes with each of them. The softness of one woman's eyes made me pray that perhaps the look was intended to give me a sign. I heard the words and planned what I would do afterward before the jury foreman even spoke.

The jury finds . . . guilty.

The minute I heard the word, my shaky hands took out a button with my baby's face on it and placed it at my heart. A button I had made for all of my family and friends who came to the trial, but was banned from the courtroom during the trial. *Guilty.* I fell to my knees on the courtroom floor with tears in my eyes. Thanking God for some semblance of earthly justice. I sat with the realization that for many in that room, it was now over. I was relieved for them. The witnesses, jury, and district attorneys all could breathe deeply and go on about their lives. But I also knew that this was no one-act play for me. There would be many more acts to come. Many more opportunities to figure out what would come next. Many more chances for me to envision my life *after*.

Ever since I was a creative little girl, I've always had a passion for visualization. There are so many times in my life when I have visualized moments before they happened. It's as if my spirit prepares my conscious self for whatever is going to happen next. Sometimes it's an incredible thing, like receiving an award for my professional work or accepting a dream job when the phone call comes. Other times, it's quite the opposite. Bracing myself for what it would mean to stand in front of shocked family and friends and read a poem at my mother's funeral. Years later, finding myself standing up in front of some of those same people and talking about my daughter. These visualizations are slightly more than just discernment. And they certainly aren't some kind of strategy. If anything, it is a survival mechanism. By going inward and allowing myself to visualize the outcome that I think will be the healthiest or safest or most desirable for me, I've allowed my mind and body to prepare for it in advance. Somewhere along the lines in my life, I learned that making it up as I go along was not a luxury I could afford. My spirit likely gifted me with this for sheer survival.

The visualization is like an internal mirror. The mirror reflects what's coming so when the devastation bears down, I'm already three or four steps ahead. After receiving that first frantic call from Gabrielle's nanny that day and falling down on my knees in that tiny conference room, my mind played out what I would need to confront what I was facing. I knew in my bones I would need fortitude and strength like I'd never needed them before. In that moment, I visualized what my next moves should be and talked myself through them.

Make sure you find out if she was at school today.
Make sure your boss knows what's happening.
Find someone to get you to your car and home.
Make sure Mrs. White knows what's happening.
Make sure she gets a ride to the scene.
Make sure that one of Mrs. White's relatives is also
    at the scene to be there for her.
Make sure family and friends know what's going on.

All of these things ran through my mind like ticker tape even as I kneeled in my own anguish. This kind of "going inward" allows me to slow down time enough to determine what I need to do and to create some emotional distance from the physicality of the horror in front of me.

So there's no particular practice I have the expertise to recommend. Just choose what works best for you. Life coaches like my dear friend Cheryl Richardson would recommend being present in your heart and not in your head. No matter how hard that sounds, you must be able to make an honest assessment of where you are in the moment. *Am I healthy? Am I okay? Is this the right move for me? How am I going to get to tomorrow?* Those questions might be first generated within the mind, but that internal mirror that reflects back the answers is very much connected to the spirit and soul. And when it's time to actually live out whatever it is, you might not be ready, but you'll be prepared. Just breathe and take the first step.

When your new dance leads you to the edge of your sanity, keep breathing.

When your new dance partner blindfolds you and tells you to keep listening for a familiar melody amid the chaos—keep moving, keep breathing. Visualize your partner. The room. Your heels. The musicians. Imagine everything you need to execute the still-unknown next steps.

This same method can be used anywhere, from preparing for a job interview or a difficult conversation to keeping calm during a big milestone you want to be sure to remember. The more you have mentally rehearsed and imagined, the more you can be present in the moment to make quick decisions about the unknown.

Visualization is your insurance policy for survival; if you've mentally been through it already, you will be better equipped to handle it when it comes in real life. Whatever happens, know that you are strong enough to cash it in when you need it. In the meantime, it doesn't matter if you know the destination, or even want to go. Just visualize the things that may bring you momentary joy, or peace, or satisfaction. And then show up in your life every day determined to get there.

— 19 —

Grasp the Sanctity of Solitude

October 8, 2017
Today is Sunday. Yesterday I ran a bunch of errands and found
myself at the mall around 6 p.m. on a Saturday night. It was
like the walls were caving in on me. Stores with children's things,
parents with strollers, tweens and teens obnoxiously strolling
and trying to draw attention to each other. How is it possible
that I will be a pioneer of my bloodline, to live past my mother's
years and tragically decades beyond Gabrielle's? I will not have a
blueprint or a guide. I will not have a shadow to share my stories,
testimonies, or wisdom with. I sojourn alone.

I don't have that common denominator of love and memory with a partner who has also experienced this loss in the same way. Some of my
memories are scattered among friends and family, nannies, and my dad
and former mother-in-law. But I do not have that true other half of
Gabrielle's DNA to reflect with me; to open her time capsule that we'd
put together many years ago. Of course I have a village. But that village
can only go so far. They walk with me to the edge of my pain as much as
they can, but there is a stretch of the journey I'm forced to travel alone.
They will certainly stand on the perimeter and wait for me to return.
But in the depth of my darkness, I walk alone.

No one else could meet with the DA after the murder. No one else could identify Gabrielle's body. No one else had to rise in front of thousands of people, dressed in white, and proclaim that she would not be destroyed.

There are some journeys in our lives we can only take alone. That fact can often cause feelings of isolation or being overwhelmed. Instead, I challenge you to find the sanctity in your solitude. Use moments away from the noise and chaos of everyday life to focus on the quiet and hear the whispers of your soul. I cherish my relationships with friends, family, and colleagues. I value the advice of trusted confidants. However, there are decisions and direction I will only find within. I love the "hero's journey" in comparative mythology. It is the common template of most of the stories we read or watch on television and film. It involves a hero who goes on an adventure, is victorious in a decisive crisis, and comes home changed or transformed. There is a path from the familiar to the unknown, and encounters with mentors and the supernatural. There are also challenges or temptations. If you think of the hero's journey as a 360-degree circle, you can imagine the hero at the top, and as he travels down and around the circle, he descends into the deep darkness—an abyss—at 180 degrees, the polar opposite of his *before*. It is dark in this place—literally or figuratively. The contrast of light bouncing against the darkness is where revelation happens. Our hero will then travel back up the circle, clockwise. Transformed. Reconciled with his past and past mistakes. Back from the unknown to the known.

My goal isn't to give you a basic Mythology 101 lesson. My goal is for you to see yourself as your own hero. We each have a journey that is inextricably connected with so many others. Some we encounter briefly, accidentally. Others we will walk with for most of our lives. Yet, there are moments in our lives when we'll also stand alone. Walking stick in hand. Backpack sagging against the weight of all we are carrying. Some of us look for any distraction to avoid our solitude. To evade the screaming silence. We fear being alone. We fear being isolated. We fear what we don't know.

When I wake up in the middle of the night, it's just me and Barbara, Gabrielle's precious dolly. It's just me and my thoughts, fears, and memories. Fortunately, when I think about my faith, I know that I may be alone in the human realm, but I am not alone in the spiritual one. Whether I'm reminded by the sound of a cardinal, or a warm breeze, or a picture of my beloved little girl, I have a gut-level, foundational, rocklike reassurance that my God and my Gabrielle are still with me. And that blessed assurance gives me the fuel to keep going long after I am too tired to keep pushing through. My defiant faith says, yes, there are moments when I must go at it alone. Yes, there are moments that no one here on earth can share with me. And yet, just like the popular poem "Footprints in the Sand" by Mary Stevenson says, I know when I'm being carried.

When you find yourself in that stuck place, stop, breathe, and pray. Praying doesn't have to be to some divine entity if that's not your thing. It could be a meditation, a self-reflection, or a few deep breaths. For some, it's a kick-butt workout or walking in nature. Whatever it looks like, find a way to connect to your heart and your spirit and slow your mind down.

When you feel trapped, it's easy to make quick decisions or to default to the familiar even if it's not good for you. Out of pure exhaustion or frustration, you may consider choosing "the devil you know." So do not get overwhelmed by how far you have to go. Just like Job found out, misery truly loves company. People are drawn to wrecks of all kinds. The "rubbernecking" of family, friends, and associates who perhaps had no interest in personal connection before your trauma occurred can be dangerous. My own physician of more than ten years was teary-eyed when I saw her for the first time after Gabrielle's death. Even with all of her professional experience, she shockingly asked me what happened. *Why did he do it? How did he do it?* Needless to say, I now have a new doctor. I have found that my situation is so unimaginable that people sometimes come to me like wide-eyed children expecting me to somehow make sense of it for them. Even when people mean well, sometimes their "help" or attempts to put their feelings into your mouth can be problematic.

And while others don't have the right to dissect your pain in front of you, you get to ask why. You get to feel everything you feel. Remember, you can gift yourself your "crazy half hour." But self-pity is like quicksand. Once you start to sink, it's hard to pull yourself out. This is why finding a way to serve others is so critical at this juncture. The more you focus inward on your pain and choose to label yourself a "victim," the deeper into the pit you can go. You'll keep looking for things that are wrong or unfair or unjust, and guess what? You will always find them. On the other hand, when you choose to look to the horizon and shift your focus toward helping others, then the light becomes more visible from the pit. You can pivot from the "victim" of your *before* to the "survivor" and "thriver" of your *after*.

None of this means that you don't allow yourself to be vulnerable. It certainly doesn't mean that you shouldn't get help or support. I am a firm believer in therapy, and I am certain that the brilliance and compassion of my therapist, Caroline, played a tremendous role in my ability to keep going. When you are struck by grief, those around you are likely suffering as well. People who you would typically confide in might be going through their own struggles with the "aftershocks" and may not have the bandwidth or resources to provide you with the support you need. Finding a "neutral" resource like a pastor or a therapist, or even an associate who steps up in the moment, is incredibly vital.

You may learn that the people close to you are too close. Your weight and pain is naturally tied to their own. Finding support outside of your circle can be quite liberating. Sometimes mere acquaintances become kindred spirits because of the similar paths you have traveled, even if you never traveled those paths together. Be open to sharing with and hearing from new voices with fresh eyes and ears. They may be disconnected from your personal trauma enough to step back and let you completely and unabashedly unravel.

Remember that resilience is built by resistance. Your faith is strengthened by the fires. When you're in the middle of the fire, it's hard to see what's on the outside and what the possibilities are. However, those who can see the distant flames, and marvel at your ability to remain standing in them, will be impacted in ways you cannot imagine. Sometimes our struggles and challenges are not about us. I truly believe that sometimes they are a way to bless and inspire others.

Be brave enough to walk out on your own. When life's circumstances cause you to question the core of who you are, or the course of your path, it may be time to find that solitude. As painful as it was at times to be alone, having that quiet space allowed me to write. It allowed me to pray. It allowed me to hear the reassuring song of a cardinal reminding me that I was connected still to a love and life that I could no longer feel or see. If you spend your whole life running from the moments of solitude, you will never truly discover *your* personal journey. Your mission and choices will continue to be based on the needs and opinions of those around you. That is what a lot of life looks like for all of us, and that is okay. However, at the intersection of life, where you stand at the crossroads of what once was and the unknown, you can find your *yet* in the quiet. You can discover what you are really made of. You can perhaps remind yourself who you are and Whose you are without the distraction of outside voices. There are old gospel songs about "prayer closets." In some ways, when I found a small dark space to fall to my knees as my life unraveled that horrific afternoon with a phone call, I was going to a prayer closet. I was looking for a space to block out everything except for me and my Maker. In the "closet," we can wrestle with our God or the universe. We can question and cry out. Ultimately, we can begin to reconcile what once was and what may be in the future.

If you embrace these moments of solitude, if you ask the universe why you may feel alone when you want to literally run away from yourself, your courage will be rewarded. Your path may be messy and even frightening at times, but the other side is out there. Keep walking.

— 20 —

Mine Your Memories

Part of our ability to continue to have hope, to be resilient, may in fact just be part of our DNA. We can't take credit for that. We were given it. We are also taught resilience. I have such admiration for people who find their spirituality later in life. They are the ones who have actively sought out faith, who studied and read as they looked for answers. I am one of those who have faith as part of my nature. It was gifted to me from birth, and even on the Sundays when I rolled my eyes behind my mother's back about getting up early for Sunday school, a tremendous gift was being transferred to me from my parents and grandparents. Faith was my birthright. Yes, I certainly *chose* to hold on to it when I could have abandoned it. However, when my mother passed away and then her mother a few months later, I realized that it was, in fact, the only thing I knew for sure.

My encounters with death and dying began very early. The reality of life and death has sat with me my entire life. Obviously, children eventually learn that things and people die, but to have so many close experiences, so young, can be heavy. So much of that internal reluctance to be called "strong" or "supernova" has to do with who I understood myself to be as a child.

I was in first grade when my first real friend died. While it wasn't a sudden death, it felt like a sudden loss to me as a child. I was a shy kid and sometimes there would be bullies who picked on me. My friend

Willie always had my back, though. He told those kids to leave me alone, and at least for a moment, they listened. My memory is permanently seared with the scene of him taking a slap for me one cold winter morning at recess. Months later into the school year, I remember being asked to draw a picture in memorial for him because this same friend had died. I knew he was no longer with us, but no one explained much more than that.

I didn't know he was sick. I did know he had defended me from these kids. So my six-year-old brain feared that maybe I was the cause of his death. That maybe he died because he cared for me and protected me and loved me. And I held that belief for years, until, in the fourth grade, my mother caught me doodling his name with hearts. She asked me who it was, and when I told her, she seemed surprised, and I said, "I killed him. He was trying to help me and he died." She said, "No, no, no, no, that's not what happened, sweetie. He was a sick little boy. He had leukemia and that's how he died." I had carried it for all those years without that knowledge. She seemed surprised that I still was holding that. It wasn't necessarily guilt or shame I felt. It was fear. I was afraid of everything when I was a little girl. I was too tall and skinny, with teeth that were too "buck." I was also too willing to answer all of the teachers' questions. I was a central casting target for a bully. At six years old, the ability to comprehend what had happened to Willie or ask for help from someone who wasn't family, let alone someone who wasn't a grown-up, did not register. My fear was tied to the idea of one day losing something I loved. Even at that young age, in my little girl crush way, I loved Willie. And Willie died. I also feared losing my mom because I loved her so dearly and couldn't imagine how I could live without her. I didn't want her to die either.

That experience of losing my friend shaped me in ways I've only begun to understand. I was afraid that when I loved people too much they could go away. I think Willie's death also made me wary of the transient nature of love and relationship. I knew early on that things and people we loved could go away. I went to five elementary schools and two high schools. It didn't matter if we loved our old school, there would one day be a new one. Yes, we loved our old friends, but then there were new ones also. I was so young when I realized that what I'd known before could easily become no longer. So the fear of losing someone or something precious, and the desperate desire to do everything "right" to keep it or them, is likely rooted in that early trauma. The cruel irony, of course, is that as a type-A overprotective mother some forty years later, even with the best baby-proofing and literally hiring a professional car seat installer, with all the trappings and paranoia of an educated career mom, I could not have anticipated where the darkness that actualized my adult worst fear would come from.

I experienced other sudden losses during my childhood—my godfather, a teenage friend, the father of family friends who was like an uncle to me. After realizing that I'd carried Willie's death all those years, my parents took a different approach with me going forward. Their honesty and transparency about these three other losses, none of which were from natural causes, made a difference. While the scenarios and outcomes were hard to comprehend, I was able to handle the truth of what happened. I was able to separate my fate and faith from the unpredictable and unexpected turns of life. I was a survivor, not a victim or a perpetrator. These events helped give me perspective as I faced the lesser everyday challenges of life. To this day, I hear my mother's voice reminding me, "Nothing is life and death except life and death."

When I think about these early losses, I actually think I was too young to really make the link between what I was learning in Sunday school and church and my understanding of life and death. By the time my mother died, I was an adult living in an adult world and facing adult challenges. My faith at that point was much more deeply embedded in my heart and soul than I realized.

I grew up traveling to Terre Haute, Indiana, where my grandfather, "Papa," was the pastor of Second Baptist Church on Oak Street. I would be so proud when I went to my grandfather's church. We were the only family members who did not live close by, and so it was a treat to be recognized in a place where all the faces were familiar. They may not have always known my name, but they knew I was "Reverend Hord's granddaughter" and "Noel Edward's' girl." I loved standing at the back of the church with my papa and shaking parishioners' hands as if I was some sort of "deacon" at five or six years old.

My grandmother played the piano, and my dad, who had grown up singing in the church choir, would always be summoned by his mother to come up and sing. Grandma Jessie would pass a note to a church deacon, who would then typically pass the note to Reverend Hord, and then Reverend Hord would inevitably "decide" to have his son come up. One of my grandmother's favorite songs for him to sing was called "He's Sweet I Know." I remember sitting next to my brother on the wooden church pew and discreetly patting him on the side of his thigh as if to say, "Here we go!" I would proudly watch my dad walk to the front of the church as the audience encouraged him with "Sing, son!" and "Let Him use you." My father has a beautiful voice, and it wouldn't take long for my grandmother to get so excited and moved by her son's voice that the Holy Spirit would have her shouting in praise. Somehow, like out of a movie, she could still come back in on that piano and hit the right notes on time!

Back home in Michigan, my Sabbath experience did not include Sunday brunches and playdates. It was Sunday school, church, and then some fabulous soul food in the late afternoon. My mother was not only a schoolteacher, but she was also a Sunday school teacher. On special days, like Easter, we'd stay in church all day. I met Tara, my dear childhood best friend, in Sunday school when we were five and we've stayed connected ever since.

Faith was a seed planted deep in my bones and lovingly watered by my family and village my entire childhood. Church was not just somewhere we went, it was integral to who we were. I never questioned our churchgoing or religious background. And when my mother died, it all hit me. All of those years, all those lessons I consciously and unconsciously held deep in my body, were a rehearsal period. Even those early childhood losses were dress rehearsals for when I actually had to be on the stage of life. They were preparation for the moments when the universe would call upon me. I unknowingly was training for this moment my entire life and had the tools and community to get through.

One of the things that faith does, whether the "owner" realizes it or not, is testify. Without even trying or realizing what I was doing, the mere act of writing my mother's obituary, standing in front of a congregation to speak about her at her memorial service, sharing about her at our family's annual charity gala, were testimonies of faith.

I remember the first time we went back to church after my mom died. My parents had just moved to Ohio, so while it wasn't a familiar church, it was a familiar place. I do not remember the song, but a gospel hymn I knew deep in my bones was sung by the choir. I looked down and found myself patting my knee with my right hand. Both my hand and the reflex action so resembled my mother's hand it stunned me. I was unconsciously mimicking the action I had watched her do my entire life. In that moment, I crawled into my father's lap—to the extent my five feet and eleven inches could—and cried. Behind us some young women were gossiping and giggling. I watched him write with a shaky hand on a piece of paper that "her mother just died" and hand it to the girls. They went silent immediately.

That was the beginning of my discovery of how faith is both nature and nurture. In mining the memories of my life, I figured out that one of the greatest lessons I learned from losing my mother and grandmother months apart at twenty-four was how to have grace in grief. That's what those past memories will teach you. When I lost Gabrielle, grace was the muscle memory I drew upon in order to sustain the enormous waves of sorrow and rage that followed. We all must find a way to live even when we want to die. Our testimony is depending on that. It's easy, and maybe even reasonable, to forget that the strength we need to endure exists within us. But every day we wake up with breath still in our bodies is an opportunity to identify the things that will drive our resilience and to pay attention to all the ways God will show up to support us.

This is important, so it bears repeating: Everyone grieves differently and about different things. But no matter what or how we grieve, we all must learn to sit with the pain. We learn how to sit by remembering all the other times we sat. And it's in the stillness of the discomfort and in the memory of grace that we truly uncover our path to healing.

— 21 —

Embrace Your Vulnerability

March 3, 2018
I need to keep working out to keep my brain moving. Even
though my heart has stopped, little signs that I am alive continue
to emerge out of thin air. Something harmless during normal
weather becomes a deadly weapon in this storm. A cute Brownie
selling her Girl Scout cookies reminds me of Easter and an Easter
bunny. A flash of remembrance that Gabrielle's friends are
heading into the fourth grade. I don't get a forecast. I step and
stumble, minute by minute. Sometimes God's grace and mercy
show me pockets of hope. Sometimes I'm mowed down by a sharp
edge coming at me a hundred miles an hour from a connection to
what once was and never will be.

I remember coming to my grandparents' house right before my mom's memorial service because my grandmother was too sick to attend. I sat next to her on the bed and she put her hand on my leg. She said, "Well, kid, you have two choices. You either keep going or you lay down and die."

Well damn. Good talk, Grandma.

I suppose nothing says *strong* like an elder Black woman facing down the Reaper herself while burying her daughter.

I joke about that day sometimes, but in truth, what she said felt like something I'd always known. Death will come, but in the meantime we have to keep living. Every day we make a choice to engage in the world; to try. Not necessarily to succeed but to keep trying. One of the side effects of this, at least for me, is that sometimes my trying looks like victory to people. I could have a myriad of emotions going on—anger, deep sorrow, pain—but because I know how to keep going, people use me as a prototype for some kind of superhero status that feels nothing like it may look from the outside.

I was introduced to the concept of double consciousness through the book *The Souls of Black Folk* by scholar W. E. B. Du Bois. It explains the internal conflict experienced by a colonized group in an oppressive society. He describes the African American experience as one of double consciousness. I certainly understand that, in modern terms, whether one calls it double consciousness or code switching, there's something challenging about contorting yourself and creating these different facets of your personality in order to be palatable to the dominant culture. We all do it in different ways. Perhaps to fit in with the moms at school. To wriggle your way into your corporate "old boys' club." It is certainly a survival play for me as a Black woman in America. However, I think we all have different pieces of ourselves that we can pull out or put away depending on the circumstances. At times, we use our masks or armor to defend ourselves literally and figuratively. We take them to job interviews. Chris Rock once joked in a comedy special that we send our "representative" out on our first dates. This representative shows up looking like us but often sounds and operates the way we would like to be seen instead of the way we actually are.

The armor we choose to wear can be an act of defiant faith. In particular scenarios, we will choose to act in ways that may be the antithesis of what we really feel. Why? Because some days, we just want to fit in. We want to impress. We want to protest the emotional upheaval happening on the inside. We want our defiant faith to roar. There have been multiple iterations of my armor. Grieving my mother required an outward expression of my pain and grief. My Gabrielle's Wings "posture" is about fighting. It is about showing little girls and boys who look like my daughter what surviving looks like. What love and help look like. So in those moments, when I need to smile and speak publicly and perhaps hold the hand of a mother or child either here or on the other side of the world, I want to stand strong. I want to look like I am persevering and thriving. I want to wear my *yet* in bold colors on my face and in my posture.

There are other days when I need the representative I'm sending out into the world to express outward signs of the pain I am in. Not too long after losing Gabrielle, I decided to stop wearing makeup. A simple thing, I know. But not wearing makeup was a way to say, "I'm not okay." In the same way that people from other traditions wear black for three months or those from the Jewish faith sit shivah, my bare face was an outward sign of the pain I couldn't express.

I started going back and forth between the two presentations of myself, especially in those early days. Even now I am thoughtful and deliberate about which representative of myself I send out into the world.

Gabrielle's story is now the core test in the testimony of my life. A testimony that is both difficult to deliver and to hear, but which offers the hope of survival and resilience to those on the receiving end.

It goes back to that question I am asked and hear in whispers: How does she do it? I do it the way people always have. I suffer. I make mistakes. I survive. I continue to move in faith and trust that there will be ground that shows up when I drop my foot again. I give myself space and permission to feel. Grace means being open to the voices and experiences and connections that exist for us if we will only attach our heads to our hearts and dive in. We cannot watch the experience of life like a bystander. It requires us to get in the mud and on the field.

As I learned in basic yoga, I had to perfect my warrior pose. It was during this time that I figured out my warrior strength was less about fighting and more about the preparation. I needed to be deliberate about how I moved through the world, and thoughtful about how I represented myself. If I needed the world to give me a little extra space, I had to find a way to communicate that. And if the moment called for a show of strength, I needed to call upon every resource I had to summon my fiercest self. The warrior pose suggests you're ready for whatever is coming, even if you can't imagine what's next. Even as I was crushed into pieces on the inside, on the exterior at Gabrielle's service or at public events for Gabrielle's Wings, I held my warrior pose. It's an exterior shell that outwardly emanates hope, strength, and resilience regardless of what may be going on inside. In the early days of a tragedy like this, you perfect your warrior stance, say the right things, and speak the right truths with the hope that one day those truths will seep into your actual being.

Where does my grace come from? It comes from my search for the mercy of a higher power and the generations of stories I've been privileged to hear. It comes from standing on the shoulders of giants. It comes from nature's reminder that there is a continuum of time even when it may feel like it has stopped.

It is important to know how to practice self-care and withdraw to give yourself time and space. Yet, some of the most powerful moments can be missed if we aren't able to risk vulnerability and take all the armor off sometimes. Piece by cold metal piece. Sometimes we protect our hearts by withdrawing into that armor, and sometimes we strengthen the resiliency muscles of our soul by baring all. Again there is not one set playbook. Define what you need in your *yet* minute by minute and day by day to continue on your path.

My *yet* says that regardless of what I may feel in a given moment, regardless of what I've had to give away or concede, regardless of what I thought my life looked like before, I am still here. I am still trying. I am willing. I am protecting myself when I need to and exposing my vulnerability when it will help me. *Yet* is the pivot from your present situation to your future possibility. Carry what you need with you on this journey and be smart about what is too heavy to take along. It matters less how you choose to wear your armor than that you have the strength to know when you need it, and when to leave it behind so you can keep going.

— 22 —

Share What You Can

Knowing who you are also means knowing who and what you need in those crucial moments. Holding on collectively to others who share my journey so we can lean on one another, prop one another up, and even carry one another at times, if needed. Somehow I knew that Gabrielle's young classmates would give me oxygen in a way that perhaps my peers could not. Remembering the years I held on to the idea that I was responsible for my friend's death and the potential impact of that on my psyche, I decided to go to Gabrielle's second-grade classroom the week after her murder and share with them.

I was a class mom and took that role seriously. It gave me pride despite it being hard as a working mom. There were times when Gabrielle didn't understand why I couldn't hang out around the school all day like her friends' mommies. So when I could be there, I was all in. In fact, when she was in Montessori school, they would do an annual Thanksgiving Day celebration, with all the trimmings, for about forty kids; the moms were all assigned a holiday, and for sure, Thanksgiving called for an army. Enter Major Mommy Michelle. For both years Gabrielle was in the program, I would get up before dawn and get Crockpots and pans going. I'd show up with a smorgasbord of food—everything from turkey to stuffing to sweet potatoes to the best desserts. Gabrielle was so proud that her mommy had done this, and the teachers didn't seem to mind either. So when she went to elementary school, I still planned to be involved as much as possible. I couldn't go to PTA meetings in the middle of the afternoon, but I would do what I could do. I raised my hand to help with the cookie drive for Girl Scouts. I don't think being a Green Beret is any more hardcore!

I had two years with her class, and I got to know the children and their families really well. Whenever I came in, Gabrielle's little face would beam, or if one of her friends saw me first and I heard the loud child whisper, "Your mommy's here," I'd watch her slowly turn around to meet my gaze.

This particular program at her school had two classrooms of children—half native English and half native Spanish speakers—together for their entire elementary education. So I really knew these children and their parents. I felt it would have been both devastating and inappropriate for the children to attend Gabrielle's funeral. So I was determined to give them a way to acknowledge her passing and to share their love for her.

I was terrified to walk into the school, let alone the classroom, that day. Walking down the corridor and seeing the usual signs and children's art, hearing the familiar squeals, was so difficult. Even the scents of this place, where I had spent so much time over the previous three years, assaulted me. The murals on the walls signaled it was the end of the school year but felt like the markings of a tomb to me as I walked the hallways for the first time without Gabrielle. As I got closer to the classroom, the hard floor underneath my feet felt like it would collapse and swallow me whole. My fear and sorrow, however, could not override my mother's instincts to be strong, to be honest, to be loving, and to be reassuring. So I slowly kept walking.

Members of my village were with me. Silent and solemn, Desi, Darnese, Wanda, and Carmen quietly held me up by the sheer weight of their love. When I walked into the room, the children were on the rug as if it was circle time. A rug where I had watched them sit many times with my child among them, awaiting a story, lesson, or snack. The principal, teachers, and many parents were lined along the back of the room behind the kids. I sat in front of those beautiful little faces and smiled. Their little eyes were searching not just for answers, but for signs. The mother in me knew I had to let them know that their grief was real and okay even if it looked or felt very different from the weeping grown-ups behind them. I met the eyes of several children I knew personally and sent a silent message, *I'm still Miss Michelle. I am still Gabrielle's mommy. She isn't here and it is awful, but we still are.*

I showed them the beautiful tribute video that my dear friend Maureen and other friends from *Good Morning America* had shut down edit rooms to create for the funeral. It was everything Gabrielle was . . . funny, musical, bold, and full of laughter that made everyone smile. Toward the end of the video, a popular song from the movie *Moana*, one of the last movies to come out before she died, played. She loved the song, and it caused my heart to squeeze with love and pain as I heard several of the little girls sing along under their breath to the video.

See the light as it shines on the sea? It's blinding.
But no one knows, how deep it goes

I knew there was no way to normalize what had happened for me or the kids. I focused instead on what we knew for sure. Gabrielle loved to laugh. She loved to make them laugh. She knew and loved them. She loved popcorn. I called the names of a few children and brought up stories of things I knew about them because of Gabrielle and because of my time in the classroom. In my head I thought, *Yes, babies, everything has changed but some things remain.*

I shared my story of early loss in the first grade and tried to give them permission to feel the full range of emotions burgeoning in their little hearts. I wanted them to know they could be sad, confused, and angry. They could also smile and laugh at the good memories. It was critical that they were able to see that I could still stand and breathe and laugh and cry. That I was still here and they were still here and it was okay to laugh about something Gabrielle did in one breath and cry in the next. In a way, I was giving six-year-old Michelle the permission she never received back then to bare her feelings and all of the vulnerability that came with them.

I hope that somehow Gabrielle's classmates gained resilience in the midst of this tragedy. As they watched the unimaginable play out before their eyes, as they watched the "grown-ups" show fear and grief, hopefully there was a lesson buried in their souls. To embrace and accept how they feel, to express what they need, and to reconcile that some things will never make sense. I pray that my willingness to be vulnerable in front of them will empower them to do the same when life shakes them in ways they might not have imagined. We talk so much about bravery and courage and strength, but at the root of all of that is the ability to express the intimacy of vulnerability.

My next demonstration of vulnerability with Gabrielle's classmates was deciding to invite them with me when I went to spread Gabrielle's ashes. Because of our mutual love for the ocean, I decided to release her ashes into the Long Island Sound because it fed into the Atlantic Ocean where we had so many wonderful memories. After talking to several people about it, including child psychiatrists, I reached out to the parents and explained what I had in mind and why I wanted to include their families. I wanted to give everyone an outlet for their emotions, and to help show them that grief was an ongoing process that could take many forms. I needed to let them know that it was okay to be vulnerable. I wanted the children to know that grieving was okay and even necessary. That even the "grown-ups" in their lives did not have all of the answers. They needed to know that life sometimes presents tough and impossible questions and that the best anyone of any age can do sometimes is stumble through and learn what it means to survive. I wanted to give them a tangible way to express how they felt.

A friend of mine, James, who is a DJ, provided the sounds of Radio Disney for the event. I rented a boat and had a delicious array of all of Gabrielle's favorite foods: BBQ, popcorn, and cotton candy. The kids did an art project where they wrote special notes to my baby on paper angel's wings. Many of those I still have in my home. As I released the ashes from the urn, shaped like a seashell from a mermaid movie, into the water, each of the children was given a white rose to hold close and then release. Then, as we floated away from the waters littered with a floral memorial, Gabrielle's young friends danced and ate and laughed and hugged. It was a beautiful, powerful day.

•   •   •

SOME OF US were taught that if you stop looking or thinking about grief it will go away. It doesn't. Not for adults and certainly not for children. It's so important that we normalize grieving for them. Give them a wider, more layered view of what grief looks like.

As adults, we always discount the resilience of children. I think sometimes we want to think things are too complicated for them to understand, but they are observing and creating stories whether or not we participate. Children encounter loss, no matter how well-intentioned parents or caregivers may try to shield them from it. We live in a world where loss is part of the twenty-four-hour news cycle. It's uncomfortable, yes. But when we talk about it, we give our children tools that life is going to require of them anyway.

Things that are mysterious and unknown can be frightening to adults, let alone kids. We must allow them to give voice to their feelings and confusing emotions. If we don't tell children their feelings are okay, they will, like I did, hold them way too tight on the inside. Or those feelings will show up in their behavior elsewhere.

This normalization of grief for children is vital. Grief obviously can show up for many reasons, and most are not as extreme as a loss due to violence. Children need to be protected, yes. Children are also resilient and can hold more than we often allow them to. Trauma, loss, disappointments are not linear. These things show up differently depending on the person. No one has it all figured out. It took everything in me to stand in front of Gabrielle's classmates, to look into those little faces, and share my heart with them. But I did. And as a result, my vulnerability served all of us that day.

—23—
Find Your Army

I am waiting with open arms for your return. Swimming next to you. I cannot replace what you have lost, but I will love you as fiercely as I am able. Thank you for still being here. Thank you for sharing your truth in a way no one else can. I love you.
                    —email from my friend Kelly, May 10, 2019

Please take care of yourself, Sister. You have mighty things to accomplish for God's kingdom and Gabrielle's legacy. Hang on, be strong, and don't give the enemy a fighting chance to derail you. He's a sneaky bastard and you are a delicate fucking flower. I love you so much.
                    —email from my friend Katie, May 11, 2019

As warrior-strong as we need to be during the grieving process, we also have to be open to receiving the support we require. Because there will be so many moments that will catch you off-guard, it's important to build a community of people who are willing to stand with you, and then, within that community, it's important to find a core group who will truly hold you up on those days when everything freezes and you feel like you can't move.

• • •

I DON'T QUITE remember how the name started or why it was just these five people. Somewhere early in the initial hours, days, and months after Gabrielle was murdered, five of my dearest friends became my soul sisters and banded together to create my core. They were "the Five" and the nucleus of everything. They were my shield. Four out of five of them lived close by, so they took turns practically living with me. When others reached out to see how I was doing or what they could do to help, they would have to speak with one of the Five first. To this day, "Five the Hard Way" is how they are listed in my cell phone.

The Five was a group composed of childhood friends, college friends, and former coworkers. All of these women had been in my life when my mother died. Since my mother's death, several of them have lost their mothers as well. Most of them have gotten married, had children, and were there for me on my wedding day and all of the important days in between. Gabrielle was important to all of them and they were all important to her.

The rental house I was staying in during the divorce proceedings quickly became a command center. My five sister-friends Tara, Carmen, Wanda, Darnese, and Desi became the generals in my war. They led my army of love. They monitored when I needed a break from mourners and reminded me to eat and sleep when I could. They doled out my medication and kept me from, in my zombie state, accidentally taking more than what was prescribed. They helped take care of my extended family and kept a special eye on my father and brother. They made painful and awkward decisions, many of which I will never know.

So these five women bore my burdens with such grace and strength that they will forever warrant my gratitude. They went into my former home—now also a crime scene—and took discreet pictures and videos to help me pick what I would keep and what I would leave behind. They brought me a series of white dresses to try on for the funeral. Over a bottle or three of wine, I paraded around in different dresses and shoes as we pretended like we were playing dress-up for something warm and lovely and not something so terribly devastating.

Carmen's own daughter was only two weeks older than my Gabrielle. Neither of us knew we were having a girl so when she announced that she had named her baby Gabrielle, my heart sunk. A few days later, I mustered up the nerve to tell her that I didn't know what I was having yet, but that we had also decided on Gabrielle as our "girl" name. Carmen didn't miss a beat and said, "I think it would be cool to have two Gabrielles." And so we did. The girls looked and sounded like twins. They had an adorable habit of calling each other "the other Gabrielle" even when speaking to each other. This dear friend, who shared pregnancy and motherhood with me, brought several white sweaters for my Gabrielle to wear for the funeral service. I had already picked out Gabrielle's dress for the funeral. It was a white sleeveless summer dress she had once tried on and loved, but never got a chance to wear. I could have never imagined as we stood in the store, staring at her twirling reflection in the three-way mirror, that the only time she would wear it would be on such a horrific day.

While I know Tara and the rest of the Five took breaks, regrouped, and handled their own lives in between, I don't recall a single moment during that time when someone wasn't there with me 24/7.

Whenever I needed a hand, I would send a note to the Five. And once I found a trauma therapist, they met with her to try to grasp how they could be even more helpful and try to grapple with what to expect as I began the hard work of healing. Caroline let them know that there was no playbook; to be patient and know that one day I might want to be alone and the next I might want to be surrounded. She suggested they lean on one another since they each loved both Gabrielle and me and were also dealing with their own grief and shock. They more than listened and always came through.

And in those precious and protective moments that my village gave me, despite what surrounded us, we were able to laugh. Those moments were a welcome respite from the darkness. Like the time when another friend decided what food in my grief kitchen was suitable for the diet I had started before Gabrielle's murder. Or the time when my beloved sorority-line sisters started fussing on the group text about what everyone should wear for the funeral.

"We should wear all pink."

"No, I say we wear all green with pink accessories."

"Um, maybe we should wear all black. It is flattering, and everyone has a black dress."

As three of my line sisters, who were inducted into the sorority with me, sat with me in those early days, I watched them try to field the text chain. When my nosiness got the best of me and they told me what was going on, I suggested that they write back and tell everyone that I had requested they wear bright red dresses and Jackie O–style pillbox hats. We giggled as we watched the responses to see who would take the bait. I think this was my way of letting them know that despite the holes in my body and pain in my heart, there was still a little of the old me left.

It was one of the Five who initiated a weekly prayer call on Sunday nights. The call went on every week for two and a half years. It carried me through the early days, the holidays, and the literal and figurative trials and tribulations. Sometimes there were four people on the call and sometimes there were forty. No matter what, we cried and prayed together. Some longtime friends and some perfect strangers who only knew one another by voice and name came together to share their faith and pray about my fate.

I don't know if I'd ever known women so loving, so invested in the well-being of another woman, until I was faced with needing these ladies. They held back their own family challenges and stresses to focus on me. It would take a long time for me to have the strength to offer any reciprocity to these beloved sisters, but they understood and were willing to stand with me in every way. They stood with me literally or virtually for every court hearing. They held me down in ways that are still being revealed.

Beyond the Five, I have an amazing community of support. Not one village but several from different parts of my life. There are my Howard University friends from my time on the drumline. There's the Alpha chapter sorority sisters who pledged Alpha Kappa Alpha Sorority, Inc., with me or before me or after me. There are also high school friends and work friends and fellow mom friends. I've often jokingly called my community the Hord 300 or the Village People, but what these people did and continue to do is seriously amazing. Whenever they're called, they are always there. Not just day one or day five. Not just working with one another—and sometimes they were total strangers—on my behalf to arrange meals or car rides, but also ensuring I would never have to spend a night alone for the first couple of years. I relied on them for everything.

When I decided to throw a fiftieth birthday party in early 2020, just weeks before our lives changed forever with COVID, nearly fifty people came to Cancún with me to celebrate. It was a loaded birthday for so many reasons. My mother died shortly after her fiftieth birthday. Hank and I always said that we would wait until my fifty-first birthday to celebrate the milestone. But as I looked at the intersection of *before* and *after* that I faced in that moment, I heard the voices of my mother and Gabrielle. I remember hearing clearly, "Your entire life *cannot* be a memorial." So much of my adult life had been dedicated—and would always be dedicated—to the loving memories of my mother and daughter. The "nudge" that I felt from above challenged me to not get stuck in my *before*. Only I could pivot into *yet* and ultimately try to create a new *after* life for myself. So, somewhat against my will, I called in the village to celebrate a hallmark birthday minus all of the benchmarks that my peers had at that point. And they came. As they have every day and with every ask.

I have been floating through the last several years of my life emotionally like someone who has fallen in the crowd at a mosh pit. I have been carried faceup in the dark by a variety of hands. Some more stable than others. Some higher and some lower. But I have learned to trust there will always be another set of hands. And I haven't fallen to the ground yet.

SEVERAL MONTHS AFTER Gabrielle's murder, her Girl Scout Brownie Troop 2988 planted a weeping cherry blossom tree in her honor at her school. It stood steps away from where we would eventually break ground on Gabrielle's Playground. It was a poignant choice. Gabrielle loved both weeping willow and cherry blossom trees. In fact, whenever Gabrielle saw the quick and amazing burst of cherry blossoms in the spring, she had a cherry blossom song that we would sing together in glee.

One of the things the girls did during the dedication ceremony was take a ball of yarn and have each girl standing in the circle share a memory of Gabrielle. After each girl finished, she would then throw the ball of yarn to someone across the circle. In the end, there was a spiderweb of haphazard, random and beautifully overlapping yarn between the girls. A tangible sign of how their memories and connections held them together.

This idea of being grounded in relationships at such an early age wasn't something that came naturally to me. I went to five elementary schools and moved across the country halfway through my sophomore year in high school. I had to learn how to plant seeds quickly and find fertile ground for relationships over and over. I marveled at people who had lived in the same house or the same community their whole lives, because it was so foreign to my existence. So I sought ways to tether myself, whether it was within my family, or with my best friend Tara as we grew from kids in Michigan to long-distance phone calls to our collective years at Howard and beyond.

One of the most precious things about my Howard University college experience was the relationships I made there and that I hold on to today. We chose one another as young adults. We shared our fears with one another. We shared our hopes and dreams; our mischief and young heartbreaks. We chose one another before there were spouses or careers or children. If I were to run down the names of the "300," I'm sure most of the people came into my life through my college experience. It was so central to my peace and joy and sanity to have this collective of people who are not just in my memories but also in my heart and present reality.

You might read this and say, "I want a 300!" Like anything, relationships are about hard work, intentionality, perseverance, and sacrifice. Whether it is 300 or 3, whether it is people or Peloton, God or nature, we absolutely must find ways to be tethered to things beyond our mere existence. Things that bring us back to earth when we want to float away from reality. Things that hold on to us when it feels like the earth is falling out beneath our feet or some violent wind could literally blow us away. Be intentional. Decide what you need to be tethered to. Hold on to things that are worth fighting for.

As I watched Gabrielle's classmates toss the yarn back and forth in no particular pattern, but in a perfect design, it spoke to the intentionality and sometimes randomness of how and who we tether to. Could I have ever imagined being tethered to Barbara, Gabrielle's baby doll? How about to guys I was on the drumline with in college? At different points and in different moments, they have all held incalculable value. Those connections move back and forth like that yarn, across the landscape of my life. Each one tethering me to something stronger. Classmates, former coworkers, neighbors, all woven together to sit and represent Gabrielle in court in ways I could not. People who introduced themselves to my father after train and plane rides to sit in silence on hard benches all day.

Be clear: In order to have that kind of tethering, you must do your part. I take love, friendship, and commitments seriously. I remember birthdays. I have cooked for, laughed with, and shared space and memories with people who matter to me. Like faith, these relationships are a policy where I paid my premiums, and so when the unimaginable happened, I was able to cash in. We all have unique strengths and gifts to share. The more you open your heart to share yours, the more you will find blessings of grace and love return to you.

It is the frailty of love, commitment, and friendship that makes all the difference in this life journey. You build something despite not knowing when or if you will ever need it. You invest in others not knowing who you will change, who will reach out, who will make a difference for you. Ultimately, those investments can pay off with rich dividends.

Whether I'm talking about a Bible story or someone I have produced a story about, the most powerful tales are the ones where you are allowed to dig beneath the surface to see a person's vulnerability and courage. When you have the chance to see not only their final destination or ultimate achievement, but all of the steps, missteps, setbacks, and redirects that happened to get them there. For example, you might marvel at a beautiful piece of music and commit all of the words to memory. Yet, if you understand the artist's motivation, the story behind the story about all the mistakes and challenges it took to produce what you now love, you cherish it even more. As they say in elementary math, "show your work." When you see the equation for how someone constructed the melody and those lyrics, you can hold greater space for the beauty and magic of the music.

My father always says he's grateful for my faith and my fight. In addition to that, I am grateful for my family. Certainly for my biological family, but also for the people who put their lives aside to take part in mine, even on the very worst days. Many had been a part of my college life, and others had walked with me as colleagues. Most of them only had me in common but somehow that was enough. Love and loss were powerful equalizers; common denominators.

How could I repay a former boss who traveled for hours on the train to go with me to prep for the grand jury hearing? A married mother of two and professional physical therapist, driving an hour each way to give me free massages? Another former boss who generously donated the funding for the majestic Gabrielle's Playground that now sits at the front of Gabrielle's elementary school? The home cooks who provided endless meals? The chauffeurs? The sisters—not by blood but by bond—who lived hundreds of miles away but still sent selfies of themselves with no makeup and wearing a Gabrielle button as a sign of solidarity whenever I had to go to court? Those who helped me move? Create a new will? Pick an urn? There is no way for me to ever "pay back" the courage, pain, sacrifice, love, and countless hours that family, friends, and mere associates generously gave to me. However, through this journey I have learned the gift of receiving in complete vulnerability and gratitude, knowing that I would in turn offer what I could to others when called upon. I don't know that you can calculate love and kindness in a way to create "equity." I do believe in the cooperative idea. We all give what we can when we can. We all take what we need when we need it. I believe love and kindness are best expressed and exchanged this way.

I had a morning ritual that sustained me in those early days. I would wake up before the sun rose above the horizon, and in the dark I'd sit outside with my Bible and journal. Out there, in the still of the dawn, I would hold and rock myself as I cried for my baby. I would write and wait for my cardinal. The writing I did there varied depending on the state of my heart, but one thing I committed to was to send the Five an inspirational reading or motivational paragraph every morning. It was a way of giving something back, of tethering myself to them. It often required me reading several different ones to find something that felt illustrative of my current walk or connected to something I knew one of them was struggling with aside from the loss of Gabrielle. In those early days and weeks and months, it was a way of me letting them know where I was emotionally. As time went on, I had the emotional space to also focus on finding inspiration or testimonies that spoke to their experiences.

To this day, I still send those messages every day. It has now become a part of my daily routine. I still read through several devotionals every morning and try to pick something appropriate for where I am or where my friends are in life. For a long time, the devotionals were testimonies I was not yet far enough along in the process to give. They represented the hope I had that my defiant faith was leading me somewhere. Each word in those devotionals confirmed the insurance policy of faith that I held desperately in my trembling hands, trusting it would come through.

I don't know who you are or what you're going through in life. I don't know what has drawn you to my story or this book. What I do know is that you need a village. It doesn't have to be large, but it has to be strong. You need a group of empathic people from diverse backgrounds, with diverse ideas and points of view, who have the ability to hold you and one another up when necessary.

I have a friend. Not just any friend, a friend who has lost everything. I met her after the fire ignited in her life and have had to watch from afar as she stands in the middle of its uncontrolled burn. I have prayed for her every day since we first met, begging God to stop the onslaught. The pain she endures every minute of every day squeezes my heart and never goes unrecognized by me and never without tears.

I have seen her protect and love other children, I have watched as she locks eyes with them and listens intently to what they say, and I have witnessed her standing up in front of a room of strangers sharing her story in a way that was not to garner sympathy, but rather to remind all of us that God is in control.

I sometimes wish I had never met my friend because it is only due to her tragedy that our lives crossed. Of course, I wish this had never happened to her and if it hadn't, she and I would not have been at the same place at the same time. But as she reminds me, God is in control, His will be done. This did happen to her and in response, God has given her a new mission.

I may not always have the right words to encourage her. I may tell her too often how strong and amazing she is, simply because these are facts. She is love. She is grace. She is kindness. She is saving lives. She is just going to have to learn to accept awe and admiration from those witnessing her strength.

I love my friend whom I wish I had never met.

—letter from my friend Katie, June 2, 2018

If you don't have those people in your life now, challenge yourself to create some of those bonds. We spend so much of our lives now on social media creating personas and curating a vision of our lives that may or may not be true. I encourage you to seek out intimacy within your sphere of influence and immediate family, even if it's something as small as sending a thought-provoking note. Being a good friend is the best way to make a good friend. Asking questions is a wonderful way to start a conversation. Sharing something real and tangible of ourselves with others, beyond the veneer we present online, shows our vulnerability and so increases our accessibility. Your community doesn't have to be based on geography, but it may be. What is important is building that cooperative of love and kindness. Tethering yourself to it and sharing what you can when you can, knowing that, in turn, this community will also be there for you. The truth is, you never know when you'll need this support. And you can never imagine what people will do to root for hope and love. I know firsthand that there are people who will sacrifice for you. They will extend you the random acts of kindness and generosity that help you make it through. In the end, we're all just sojourners through this land. And sometimes our maps stop working. Or the compass in our hands breaks. Tragedy and grief can send us wandering. Only our fellow journeymen can help us find the next path. Embrace the ones who can hold the flashlight and sometimes give you a little glint of their own light so you can see your way. They will stand with you as you build the courage to let go of the *before*, clutch your *yet*, and move to your *after*. My faith is my North Star, but my village people are the ones who keep me going.

Lean in, my friend. Don't hesitate to ask for what you need right now. Know that some people will not know what you need until you tell them. And, in truth, your needs could change by the hour. So check in with yourself often and don't hesitate to communicate what it is that you need to get through. Let others support you to the extent that works for you, and let that pave the way to finding opportunities where you can support them that make sense for where you are. Also be willing to ask for help you can't describe. Allow others to think for you and feel with you for a season. The true miracle is that in those precious moments, you not only gift yourself with support, you gift your village with connection. You offer them affirmation that they matter, and can still make a difference. You quietly tell them that you know they are still here. Your test, your lot, may be what the universe will use to change the life of someone else. Don't you dare miss the moment.

— 24 —

Ride the Rails

Often in corporate America, expressions like "drinking from a fire hose" or "building the train and the track at the same time" come up within discussions of change management. My days in the world of corporate media afforded me the ability to see and say those clichés often. Mergers. New teams. Layoffs. I was a part of huge change management initiatives where I might see the whole picture but I couldn't share it all at once with my team. I learned in those experiences that when things are volatile and people feel vulnerable, you lead with humanity. Change first the things that stabilize the ground, as opposed to shaking up previous ideas and structures all at once. Find your "stakeholders" and "partners" who will buy in early and help you achieve the goals. Recognize that everyone processes information—both good and bad—differently. While there is no exacting equation, you can make decisions in a professional environment where outcomes are mapped out twelve, twenty-four, even sixty months in advance and then you work toward those goals. However, it looks and feels much different when you have to apply change management principles to your personal experiences. Life is not linear. Much as with our ideal weight, our bank account, or our career, our confidence does not always grow to a larger and larger crescendo of realized expectation. Closure is very much the same thing. In fact, for me part of my "letting go" has been realizing that there are aspects of my life and my journey that will never have closure. Things that will never end with an "aha" moment or tied up neatly in a bow.

My parallel tracks of trauma and the trials of regular daily life sometimes intersect and sometimes seem completely disconnected. This is where focusing on the small victories matters so much. The train derailed, but you're still a traveler who needs to get up and go. No, things don't look like you expected, but that doesn't mean you have no control over what they will look like going forward. Yes, the life you knew is gone, and no, there are no replacements. And yet, you may still find a new life waiting for you if you let go and watch where the road takes you.

My journey has certainly not afforded me the luxury to be singularly focused on any one thing. When every aspect of your life is upended, it can be extremely difficult to sort through the responsibilities to even know where to start. But you begin somewhere, and gradually a rhythm begins to emerge. Getting through the grand jury hearing and seeing a picture of my old house, the crime scene, for the first time? Victory. Leaning in to my needs and asking Phyllis, a former ABC News executive and boss, to accompany me while the DA prepared me for the grand jury hearing? Victory. Crawling out of bed after no sleep to take a shower and go to midtown Manhattan for work? Victory. Shutting the door to that Manhattan office and crying after an unexpected delay or surprise in my legal nightmares? Victory.

Closure is not a destination; neither is moving on. It's not a period at the end of your "sentence." It is more likely a conjunction or a comma. Healing and moving on can seemingly disappear as quickly as they both show up. That shouldn't stop you from looking in the mirror and telling that reflection that you did it. Whatever "it" is in that moment. It doesn't mean you won the war. It may not even mean you won the battle. But it does mean you showed up and fought. You didn't back down. And you'll fight another day.

Embracing your *yet* doesn't mean that your *before* disappears overnight. Sometimes you might feel like you are riding between those two out-of-control "trains." Hold on! You are learning a new skill—one you might not have asked to learn, but you will learn it. Pay attention to the train, and to your reaction to the bumps that may be bruising you each day. You are learning how to balance, and one day, you will realize that you've learned how to steer.

—25—

Reclaim Your Life

Seven years that you were with me
A prime number bond that can't be divided
Magical energy; Joy uncontained
And wisdom beyond just seven short years
The profound quiet of your absence
Now filled occasionally by the cardinal's song
Seven visits from the tooth fairy
Before the sparkle and fairies were gone
—Excerpt from "Seven," a poem I wrote for Gabrielle
on what would have been her eighth birthday

In addition to anniversaries of important dates, social media algorithms can trigger unexpected feelings at any time. During the criminal trial and the divorce proceedings, I abandoned all of my social media platforms. I returned to Facebook after the criminal trial ended in late 2019, and found myself contending with all the Facebook memories. It was as if the posts of my former life were pulling me back like quicksand into my *before*, as I fought to keep my feet planted in my *yet*. On any random day, things still pop up in my feed, despite many attempts to manipulate the settings. Navigating the emotional roller coaster when images would flood my timeline required me to call on grace in a new way.

It wasn't the pictures of Gabrielle that bothered me. While bittersweet, I welcomed her beautiful little face and reminders of treasured moments and events. What was harder were the memories of my marriage. Facebook reminded me that September 29, 2020, would have been my thirteenth wedding anniversary.

As I scrolled through the photos and videos, the sunny September 29, 2007, wedding and its memories felt suspended somehow between an intangible former world and an inconceivable current one. The woman in those pictures was gone. The life she planned for, prayed for, loved for, struggled for, sacrificed for was gone.

Yet . . .

I am starting to see fuzzy shapes and blurry colors; an outline of a new life with new possibilities. If I step back for a moment from my grief, I can see a mosaic taking shape with hints of familiarity. Yes, everything was blown apart. But somehow my faith and my fight are forming something new from the billions of pieces left behind. In bits and scraps of colored glass I find traces of my memories and hopes and identity-defining relationships. The things that made me. Now, I must somehow collect what I can, discard what I must, and move forward to see what else may be formed.

I chose to share that moment of pain and vulnerability on social media along with a photo from my wedding. A photo that used to be one of my favorites, it was a beautiful black-and-white closeup of Hank and me laughing. After carefully cropping him out of the picture, I posted what was left behind, both visually and spiritually. As it says in Isaiah 43:19, "For I am about to do something new. See, I have already begun! Do you not see it? I will make a pathway through the wilderness. I will create rivers in the dry wasteland."

What blessed me even more than being able to grasp the grace that grief and trauma taught me in that moment was the support I received after the post. The universe seemed to be signaling that my "insurance" policy of faith was still active. And my village reminded me that they had remained, to encourage and cheer me on again during this new phase of my journey.

You're here for a purpose and even your eloquent memory is touching people in ways you don't imagine. Keep pushing, Michelle. You have an army behind you praying you through.

—Jennifer

Follow the light. It is there. Such beautiful vulnerability. Such strength. Keep your hand on the guide rope and be persistent. Ase.

—Sonia

From the ashes, a phoenix has risen. And you are beautifully and powerfully remade. God has a wonderful purpose in store for you, Michelle! Gabrielle may be gone from the physical realm, but her spirit lives strong and thrives through you.

—LaShawn

Welcome back. You have become an instrument of God's strength walking on earth. Whatever your reasons, I am just so glad to see you back, a little at a time. It means that you still own your destiny. You are a warrior. We are only the mere mortals who have the good fortune to have been blessed by proximity to you and your works.

—Kyle

I feel that beautiful woman in the photo morphing and healing and courageously reinventing. I think those of us who are lucky enough to have it, eventually lose that raw joy of youth. I've never seen an iconic picture quite capture it like yours. Unabashed happiness. We all yearn to feel like your picture again. Then life knocks the giddy out of us all, though not quite as sharply. Thank you for your post that helps us reflect on pain and healing. Your words are like poetry.

—Shelley

People in and around my life were rooting for my reemergence. I was buoyed by the encouragement and able to see the anniversary of my marriage with new eyes. I could identify the grace of God on a day that should have kept me bound in sorrow. September 29 meant one thing to me thirteen years ago. It now meant something else. It was emblematic of change and reinvention. It symbolized the shape-shifting nature of not just grief but joy. That the joy I experienced on that day could be transformed through tragedy into "a new thing" altogether.

But there are other ways that I've been able to see and hold grace through my trials, large and small. In some cases, grace is a very tangible thing. We literally hold on to something that makes us feel strong, supported, and connected to what we love about ourselves and the people who gave our lives value. For me, grace has a name: Barbara.

When I was a little girl, the dolls that were available on toy store shelves never looked like me. Mass-market doll makers didn't seem to have any interest in replicating the nuances and complexities of real women and girls of all races. But by the time I had my own little girl, Gabrielle, the world had changed a bit, and I was so delighted that Santa brought her a dolly that looked just like her for Christmas when she was just four months old. There was never a time that Gabrielle didn't remember Barbara being in her life.

When we first got her, Barbara wore a dress with a name tag on it. Her name was special to me and my baby girl. The precious dolly shared her name with one of Gabrielle's grandmothers as well as with the baby nurse who helped me at home when Gabrielle was born. The doll became known around our house as "Little Barbara" and even had her own theme music that I created to my daughter's delight and sang to her whenever she requested it, which was often. After a few years, Barbara became a nudist. Not sure why except that maybe she and Gabrielle had some secret agreement that doll clothes were not the best in fashion.

Barbara was an integral part of our family. She and Gabrielle had matching pajamas, Halloween costumes, and Christmas dresses. When Gabrielle starting walking and talking, she would burst into the master bedroom with just the top of her cotton-candy puffs of brown hair visible above the mattress line and declare, "Bun!" She wanted a hairdo just like Barbara's as soon as she woke up.

Being a morning show news producer felt like excellent motherhood training. Television producers have to be very organized. This means you have plans A through Z lined up because in live TV, for sure, *something* is going to hit the fan. You make plans only to have them changed, broken, altered, or adjusted. And you roll with it! We have to think on our feet. We have to be grace under fire in scenarios with high stakes, and despite how fast our adrenaline is flowing. If you have to book guests, especially those in unusual or difficult situations, you have to know how to connect with people and get information, so a heart of compassion is nonnegotiable. In television news, it's important to be a quick study and have a natural curiosity. You may have just hours to get "read in" on a difficult topic and figure out how to break it down on TV.

All of these "skills" served me well as a mom. From pregnancy on, we are learning new things every day. We are planning and prepping even though the scenarios will likely look different than we imagined. Your child changes and morphs all the time, and just when you think you "have it," they shift again—physically, emotionally, psychologically—right before your eyes. My love of producing big events also meant that my kid's birthday parties were my most magnificent productions.

So that hyper-organized mind of mine went to work when Gabrielle arrived. Even before she was born, I armed our house with every piece of baby-proofing plastic, from locks to knobs, known to man. In like fashion, I had three Barbaras that I would swap out so I could occasionally put one in the washing machine, or in the event of Barbara being left in the car or in the store. We were ready for everything, I thought.

Gabrielle did eventually discover the other Barbaras, by the way. She decided one was the evil twin, Selina, and the other was . . . well . . . another nudist doll named Barbara.

Everyone in our lives knew Barbara. Gabrielle's physician would always ask to check Barbara out first during checkup appointments. If Gabrielle settled into bed for the night and asked, "Where is Barbara?!" a full-fledged investigation of the whole house would ensue until she was rightfully back in her arms.

As children become older and more aware of the world, different kinds of security blankets become more important. Things like physical and emotional safety and financial security take up more space in our minds and hearts as we grow up. I knew that my life was a painting of womanhood that Gabrielle would study closely as she became a young woman, and it was clear to me that the tapestry of my marriage was flawed and warped in ways I did not want her to emulate.

As my husband and I slugged it out over silly things like money and possessions, the multiple Barbaras became increasingly important to Gabrielle's sense of stability. One was permanently at my house and the other dolls were permanently at our family home, where her dad lived.

After she was murdered, I started sleeping with the remaining Barbara. There was only one Barbara now since the police had to comb through Gabrielle's bedroom to collect any bits of evidence that surrounded my angel in the bed at her father's house, including the other Barbaras. Barbara was now the last thing I'd hold that had also held Gabrielle.

I placed the one remaining doll snug in Gabrielle's arms during her funeral as people passed by. So many were broken by the vision of my beautiful sleeping angel snatched away too soon. I wanted Barbara there so people could see her with Gabrielle the way they remembered. As I stood with the undertaker to close the casket, I gently kissed my daughter and took Barbara. I clutched her close to my heart. I knew that with all the angels and ancestors that flew alongside my baby girl, she no longer needed this security blanket.

But I did.

Today, Barbara lives in my bag. I take her with me. In fact, she is sitting next to me as I type these words. I keep her close to remember the joy and smiles that she brought my baby girl. Like the times I snuck her into Gabrielle's backpack when she went to school on the first day each year. Or how we seriously contemplated whether it would be okay if she still wanted Barbara with her when she went away to college. Everywhere I go, everything I do, includes Barbara. She is carefully tucked next to me as I sleep, or in a purse during therapy sessions. She travels with me to see my attorney or on trips to the doctor. She's flown secretly on airplanes with friends who were desperate to try to break my nightmare temporarily with the ocean's breeze.

When I slowly started back to work and met with my team of eighty-plus people around the country on multiple conference room screens, I tried to get through the introductory sentences without my voice cracking too much. Unbeknownst to them, Barbara was next to my knee in my bag.

I don't know how long I'll need Barbara. Perhaps the rest of my life. Or maybe there will come a day when I forget to bring her somewhere and suddenly realize that the security blanket of Gabrielle's love is still so spiritually present that I no longer need it represented in physical form. I have no way to know. But for now, Barbara is a soft, consistent, smiling brown reminder of a time of dreams and promise and safety and love. Barbara is my saving grace; a security blanket that's a constant reminder of my daughter. She's that something tangible that remains. I have never washed her because I can still smell the salty sweat and tears of my baby in her fabric. It is an umbilical cord to my *before* whenever I need it.

We all need these tangible reminders of God's presence and support. Barbara is my grace in doll form, and I'm grateful to be able to keep her close in discreet ways. You probably don't have a nudist rag doll at your side, but we all need a Barbara at some point in our lives. When you grapple with loss of confidence, identity, focus, or anything else, give yourself the grace to create your own security blanket. Remind yourself that you deserve something to hold on to; something of real mass and weight that proves your senses still work. Something that tethers you to the ground and enables you to keep walking your path.

I CAN'T TALK about how to find grace as we reclaim our lives without talking about the grace Giver. I would not be here to write any book without the knowledge that there is a God in heaven who sustains me daily. A higher power who shines a light toward a new path and a new place if you are willing to keep walking. I take great comfort from thinking about another journey of promise from a passage in Exodus.

You don't have to be a Bible scholar to know the story of Moses parting the Red Sea. Whether you heard it in Sunday school or saw it in an old movie sitting at your grandmother's feet, you likely have some familiarity with the basics. The Israelites are enslaved. Moses leads his people out of Egypt. The Pharaoh decides he isn't crazy about losing his unpaid workforce and comes with an army to bring them back. Eventually Moses's faith and obedience help him part the sea so they can get to the other side.

While the miracle of the parting waters is certainly what is most often focused on when it comes to this story, there is another piece that can help us put this grief journey into perspective. Consider that place between Pharaoh and the Red Sea. It is a story of free will and freedom. It symbolizes that place in our lives when we decide to walk away from what's holding us back, with the faith that beyond our obstacles, there is somewhere better to go. When you begin to walk away from pain, ideas, relationships, and sickness, fear and the possibilities of the unknown have a way of holding you hostage. They cloud your ability to see grace or salvation in any form it might take. It's the reason why the Hebrews complained to Moses. They couldn't see where they were going, but they knew what they'd left. When we decide to follow something or someone away from our pain, when we leave our *before* and begin walking in the direction of our *after*, just as it did for the children of Israel, it can create a moment of panic. They were being led into the promised land, but as the danger appeared, the minute those chariots began to ride up, they began to cry out. They began to long for Egypt. They began to ask themselves and one another out loud whether the safety of a known slavery could somehow be better than the uncertainty of a potential freedom.

Yes, from thousands of years away, it might be easy to judge them. Why did they freak out? Didn't they know that God was orchestrating it all? Didn't they believe?

Do you?

Nothing was stopping the Hebrews from turning around themselves. From removing themselves from the covering of Moses's leadership. They were afraid and questioning, and yet they chose to press on. They decided to follow Moses's direction. And this is where I've been able to understand this season of *yet* and *after* that is upon me. The Hebrews were asked to do two things at the same time. They were to trust God enough to move forward, all while they waited and stood still.

Life sometimes requires this interesting paradox. We must have the courage to leave behind something tangible for a different life, a new normal, that we cannot yet see. This is certainly what it means to reclaim your life. But we also must be able to be still long enough in that *meantime* to hear the directions from our Creator for how to navigate to a place of lightness. When we look back at what we've been through, it can sometimes feel like walking away meant leaving everything and everyone behind. I have certainly struggled with that at times on this journey. If I try to move forward, does that mean I am somehow leaving my life as a mother behind? How can I smile or laugh again? How can I do things like wear makeup again? Will these gestures suggest to the world that my mourning has been replaced with a new morning? How can I dare look for peace or love if it means I have to walk away from myself to find it?

Sometimes you want to run away but are afraid to leave—all at the same time. I will never again drive past the home where Hank carried me over the threshold after our wedding and carried Gabrielle's car seat into the house carefully for the first time as we came home from the hospital. The last time I saw that house, it was through flashing lights and police tape. In fact, my pulse quickens when I even drive close to that block where I built dreams that were turned into nightmares. Yet, I have moved on. Through divorce proceedings and a long criminal trial process, over the course of two and a half years, I could have easily continued looking backward. There were many times when I thought, *If I walk away, what else do I leave behind?* The process of fighting to find light in a sea of darkness has also included the ritual of counting every Tuesday. At this writing, there have been 177 Tuesdays since my daughter was murdered. I find myself asking: If I don't wear my pain like a badge, how will people know? How will they remember? Will I somehow be letting go of a little piece of Gabrielle as I walk away from the dusty despair of the desert and into the sea of the unknown?

But here's the important thing: I don't desire to "live" in this space.

Much as for the children of Israel, there isn't a yellow brick road in front of me. There isn't a GPS setting on my phone that shows the destination of "HEALED" or provides guidance on how long it will take to get there. There is only a vast unknown. One that could be dangerous. One that is certainly heartbreaking. One that could drown me if the waters roll in fast and high enough. But the power of standing in God's grace and accepting His salvation is how I choose to proceed. I have decided to try. I choose every day to hear my faith and my baby girl implore me, "Keep moving, Mommy. Don't worry about where you are going. I am always going with you. I am always going to be with you. You can't forget because I am a part of you."

I have turned my head from the *before* of my personal Pharaoh and the army of memories, pain, and desperation that press toward me. Not because I think I can leave it all behind, but because I know there is somewhere else I am supposed to go. I have fled the scene with only the bare essentials, like a family escaping a house on fire. My knees are wobbly. My destination is not clear. But I have determined it is time to walk.

Maybe you are between your own Pharaoh and Red Sea at this very moment. You may hear a voice whispering to you, "Well, at least it is the devil you know!" Or, "What if you drown? How can you be sure you are heading the right way?" Sometimes the only right way is forward. Not left or right. If you can find a compass to point you in the direction of a new life, use it. You may need to recalibrate often, and that's okay. If you feel alone, find a talisman to carry with you on the next leg of your journey—just make sure it is not one that slows you down with its weight.

Of course I can't know what your Pharaoh is or what sea needs to part for you to get to the other side. But I'm praying that these words encourage you. Borrow my confidence. Keep breathing. Know that you will always have what you need and that the future you deserve—even if you do not yet desire it—is on the other side. It may even be that you have to wade into the shallow end of the sea before the path dries for passage. But don't stop. The waters will part. There isn't a scenario where going backward can lead you to your future. Whatever you leave behind will only give you the emotional space to hold on to something new. Something precious. Perhaps even something beautiful.

There are so many ways to describe this experience. We all know the popular expressions: "Between the devil and the deep blue sea" or "Between a rock and a hard place." On one hand, we have a person, circumstance, or entity that we know for sure is not good for us. That could be harmful and perhaps has been harmful in the past. On the other side, there is something else. The challenge is, we don't quite know what that something else is. It's a bit like the mystery door. Sure, there could be something scary there. But having faith means believing in the possibility of something amazing. When we choose to go back, we open ourselves up to a kind of Stockholm syndrome where we fall in love with and defend our captors. When we choose to forge forward into the unknown, we open ourselves up to hope in ways we couldn't have imagined. We have the best chance to claim a life that looks like nothing we've seen. But we must take a few steps on that journey in order to survive it.

Last but not least, remember that resilience is built by resistance. Your faith is strengthened by the fires. When you're in the middle of the fire, it's hard to see what's on the outside and what the possibilities are. However, those who can see the distant flames, and marvel at your ability to remain standing in them, will be impacted in ways you cannot imagine. Sometimes our struggles and challenges are not about us. I truly believe that sometimes they are a way to bless and inspire others. There is no scenario in which I believe that God hurt my child to teach me or anyone a lesson. There are absolutely evil forces in the universe. But even in the darkest, most inexplicable situations, testimonies and healing are possible.

I'm clear that there are no guarantees in my *after*. I know better than anyone that there sometimes isn't enough prep, pain, prayer, or promise to keep your *before* from being destroyed. What I once knew is no longer. I will always count the Tuesdays. I will always remember moments and madness that I want desperately to forget. I will always miss my beloved Gabrielle. I will always speak her name. I will, until my dying breath, fight through my nonprofit, Gabrielle's Wings, to be a hope warrior for other children. But I am here. I am searching. I am trusting. There will likely be bumpy roads on the journey to my *after*. And yet . . . I will fear not. And yet, I will stand still. And yet, I will proclaim that the Lord is fighting for me. And yet, I will somehow hold on to that peace that passes all understanding as I embark on the road to my *after*.

AFTER?

— 26 —

Make Space for Love

This thing we got
Makes the earth move
Makes the skies open
This thing we got . . .
Makes the ordinary extraordinary
Makes the impossible inevitable
This thing we got . . .
Rescued my soul from darkness and
placed it, gently, to bask in the
glowing black light of your love.
        —Excerpt from "This Thing We Got" by Michelle Hord

People I've met, casual acquaintances, have often asked, "Will you ever be able to love again?" There have been moments in the last few years when I've thought about it. I think the larger, more pervasive question in my mind was, *Would I ever be able to trust a man again?* In my body, it feels like I was this incredibly safe driver on the road of life who suddenly was taken out by a Mack truck. How do I ever stop looking for the truck? How do the people around me who love me stop looking for it? These are the people who, I'm sure, lie down at night, replaying over and over what they might have missed the first time. *Could I have warned her?* they ask in the dark, wondering whether they missed something or ignored something or could have done something differently to keep our collective past selves safe from the truck that barreled down on us all.

But as terrifying as it may seem to hop back into the driver's seat and take a risk on the open road—no one wants to be alone. There are parts of my journey that I will always carry in solitary grief, but there is also space for warmth, affection, laughter, and the feeling of protection that I craved and wondered if I would ever have again. I hoped somewhere in my heart to find in my *after* that there could be something more powerful than my pain and grief. I wondered if there could be a new chapter to the story. Someone who could love me and hold my hand while I continued my journey. I was frightened by the prospect of this, and yet still open to it.

That's when I found him.

In the place where sand, sea, and sky meet, the place I come back to time and time again for peace and familiarity, I encountered love in the form of a man named Axel.

Axel is a Scandinavian name that means "father of peace." It is derived from the biblical name Absalom, which has a similar translation in Hebrew. I'm seldom good with names, but because his was so unusual, I remembered it. A half-Bahamian and half-Jamaican man with a Scandinavian name. Why not?

The Bahamas is my happy place. It's a place I've visited at least annually for the past fifteen years. It is a place I've visited with friends and where I spent many precious moments with Gabrielle. I've made friends there, and as my life began to change and shift, I wondered if I could even possibly live there. Right after Hank's sentencing in October of 2019, I decided I would go for two full weeks. I had never been there that long, but I needed the time to regroup and think about life after the trial. People often talk about grief truly setting in after the funeral. For me, waiting for the matrimony and criminal trials, and all of the red tape and trauma that ensued, created a two-and-a-half-year funeral period. New pain, new rawness after the "thaw" from the frenzied years before. Not to mention painful new details from the trial. I left for this trip on October 22, 2019. I would find out months later that this was the exact day my divorce was finally granted. I had no idea when the plane burst through the clouds and soared through blue skies backed by a glorious sun that I would find anything in this safe haven of mine. I didn't even know I was looking for something, until I found it.

I sat on the beach for hours and hours. I walked slowly along the shoreline realizing that I had somehow gotten to the other side. Through my memories, I can walk in her little footsteps pressed into the water and earth she cherished. One day, as I stared into the waters, pondering how I got over, wondering what my *after* was going to look like, my future showed up.

Because I stay at the same resort all the time, I've gotten to know many of the people who work there. The staff knows my story, and they've been there for me in my darkest hours. Many have shown kindness toward me in small and large ways over the years. When the news about Gabrielle's murder first broke, I received a text from one of them that simply said, "come, we are waiting for you." When I showed up with a few close friends from the 300 in those first weeks, there were inspirational Bible verses taped to the mirrors in my hotel bathroom and flowers when I arrived. Shortly after I checked in on that trip, a few women who worked there came to my room and prayed with me. Women. Mothers. Others who knew my baby and couldn't imagine what had happened.

So my relationships there ran deep. And earlier in 2019, I'd had the opportunity to meet a new friend. He hadn't been working at the property long. He was young, funny, very attractive, and really smart. My first instinct was to go into what I call Mama Michelle mode. Whenever I meet someone significantly younger than me, I try to understand who they are and what they want to do with their life. I was so impressed by this young man that I gave him my phone number. It wasn't a flirtation at all. I had a sincere interest in who he was. I even offered to do what I could to help him if he ever came to New York. I had no way of knowing it at the time, but my future had showed up in the body of this loving and beautiful man.

On my next trip to the Bahamas, right after the trial, I brought my dad with me. We were both in need of some solace after the brutal criminal trial. One afternoon we were out on the beach and I introduced him to Axel.

As he talked with my dad, I teased him. "So you're not going to take me up on my offer to follow up?"

My dad, being proud, piped in. "You really should call her!" he said. "Google her! She is a media executive; definitely someone good to know."

As soon as my dad said this, my heart sunk. Of course, he wasn't thinking about it at the time. He was just proudly sharing the accomplishments of his daughter. But I knew. When you Google me, my career is no longer the first thing that pops up.

So when I returned to the Bahamas for my two-week visit in late October, I saw Axel pretty much daily at the property. He was working but would pause each time to talk with me. At some point, in the second week, as I watched him stand a bit longer than I thought he should have with a group of women about three hundred yards away from me, I finally saw him differently. Very differently. I had a bit of an attitude that he was engaging so much with these fellow guests. Then my mind started to race.

Girl! Have you lost your damn mind?

He's young enough to be your son!

Wasn't this supposed to be some sort of mentoring thing?

What is it exactly you think you feel?

Something switched in that moment that I can't fully articulate. We continued to have nice, benign conversations and, later, texts back and forth. One day as we stood and talked, a mother and child walked by. They must have caught my eye. I looked at him and said, "Someday I'll tell you my story."

His look back at me made it clear that he knew everything. He had taken my dad up on his offer.

"When and if you're ready. No need to rush. It really isn't necessary for you to share that with me."

Halloween is one of those trigger days. A reflection can become a grief spiral if I let it. Memories of costumes and parties and rushing home from work to ensure I could take Gabrielle trick-or-treating each year flood my heart. I had consciously made plans to be away each Halloween. This year, however, the escape was solo.

On October 30, when I saw Axel, my "tropical cocktail" nerve was especially strong. I blurted out, "Maybe we could go out and grab a drink sometime?"

Oh Lord, did I really just say that?

Could I be more inappropriate?

How many middle-aged women are hitting on this good-looking guy every day?

"That would be great!" he said.

Is that excitement on his face?

Or condescension?

I reasoned that our date would, at least, give me a way to be distracted on Halloween.

The next night I met him at a restaurant. It was a local spot that is part of a group of little waterfront seafood shacks that make up the famous Nassau "fish fry." I realized as I was arriving that I really didn't know him at all. A local friend who owns a taxi dropped me off like I was a teenage girl meeting someone for a movie.

"I will call you to come get me later," I said to my friend as I nervously got out of the taxi.

I felt my friend waiting and watching me after I got out of the taxi. I suppose he wanted to lay eyes on Axel just in case.

I was so in my head that I almost walked past him.

"Michelle?" he said nervously as he stood up.

We joke all the time about that first date. We sat outside and talked easily. Later, we made our way to the beach and sat in the darkness on the sand. As the waves crashed, it occurred to me that this man was going to kiss me. He did. I was so nervous, it was like I had never kissed anyone before. In fact, he had the gall to say, "You are a terrible kisser!" And as I looked at him shocked, we both burst into a laughter that broke the awkwardness.

One day recently he walked into my writing space and watched me typing away with Barbara perched by my side.

"I am talking about you," I teased.

"Your Honor, I am just a simple Caribbean man who was drugged by this American. I had no idea what was happening!" Axel said, with a fake victim voice.

"Wait a minute now . . ."

"I love you," he said with a mischievous grin.

I WOULD LATER learn that he had watched me closely that summer. It was more curiosity than physical attraction for him, at first. I was a single Black woman sitting on the beach with a book and a drink in hand all day. Alone and staring at the ocean. I suppose that was intriguing.

He shared with me his initial thoughts:

"I thought, why does this woman come here by herself; nonstop, back and forth?" he said. "Your intelligence revealed that you were a person of significance, but there was something heavy on you, as well. You would stare out at the sea. It was as if you were waiting for her to return to you from the beach."

He was right. There was a kind of waiting I did while I was there. This special place gave me room to hope. To pray. To dream again. I could direct my energy toward the existing light. In silence, as the wind and waves swirled around me, I could stand back from the crushed pieces of my life, and if I used a lens of love, I could somehow make out a picture of the future.

Axel said that he loved watching me. He'd give me my space but could see that I was finding my peace. I'd doze off for a while with nothing but the sound of the beach coming in and out on the shore.

"I questioned everything about you. What is this? What is her story? What's her journey? Every time you came, I got more and more interested. I started hoping and wondering when you would come back. I loved talking to you. About everything."

For Axel, everything changed when he met my dad. He had taken my father's advice. He'd typed my name into his computer and Hank's mug shot and a picture of Gabrielle and me came up. The headlines were clear. My husband had murdered our child.

"My heart dropped out of my ass," he told me about reading what happened. "I didn't even know how to process it."

I think he expected to read something laudatory about my work. To learn about the stars I've worked with or big network or film studio names that I was a part of. He certainly didn't expect to learn about my tragedy.

"I had to calm myself down for a minute because being close to somebody with this gravity of pain was so hard. To know that she was your only child. I'd already begun to care for you deeply. And to see how you weren't bitter? There was nothing ill-mannered about you; nothing but joy and overflowing generosity and compassion. To find out about the million-ton weight on your back was something."

Anything I needed at that point, he made sure I had. And our relationship blossomed in ways I could have never imagined. We were two imperfect, broken people who knew how to hold and harness each other's pain. The possibilities were endless. A man who shares my faith. A man who had also escaped his Egypt. A man who was also searching for his *after*. Each morning now we wake up and decide to keep walking together. Still no map. Still no guarantees. But we have brought what we needed for the journey, and while the destination is unknown, love is beginning to shine a pathway like the North Star on a clear autumn night.

IN MOST RELATIONSHIPS, there is a rite of passage that each party goes through once they've committed to being together. Part of that process includes meeting family, siblings, and college friends so they can give their input and/or support. For Axel, the process was a little different. He'd met my father already. But before he met with the rest of the village, the Hord 300 (he coined that phrase), there was someone else he had to meet. A little, cute, brown rag doll named Barbara.

Early on, Axel used to joke about Barbara. He'd call her a Chucky doll and say, "If she gets up and moves across the room, I'm out of here!" The fact that I could laugh about Barbara, given what she was to me, was one of those moments when I realized I was changing. That somehow, there were little bits of me that were evolving. My laughter was a sign of my *after* peeking over the horizon. Axel wasn't the reason I could see an *after*, he wasn't the cause of it, but he did make me realize that I was healing myself.

In a way, it felt like Axel already understood the significance of the doll. His joking never took precedence over the need for this tangible reminder of my daughter. Over time he grew fond of Barbara. On the third anniversary of my losing Gabrielle, we spent time alone together at the beach. I remember him looking at Barbara as tears filled his eyes. I watched the change happen. He felt Gabrielle's spirit for the first time. Later he said half jokingly and half seriously, "Me and Barbara have come to an understanding." And that was it. He now makes sure I never forget her. My heart warms every time I leave the house and Axel goes through my checklist of things I need to remember. He never forgets to say, "Do you have Barb?"

THERE ARE SPACES and holes in my heart that can never be filled. Spaces that only Gabrielle held. I feel blessed to have found someone in my *after* who has the ability to understand that and sit with whatever emotional wave I happen to be experiencing. We ride together the waves of reminders, continued legal strife, panic attacks, rediscovered pictures, and memories from my previous life. And while there are places in it where only Gabrielle can live, I am in awe of the expansiveness of my own heart. Hope and faith can work together secretly and create new spaces where new people can come in and help you heal. Hope and faith can reveal gaps that were always there but that you ignored because it seemed impossible for them to be filled. These spaces have always included morning prayers and hard work and determination and family. They now also hold a kind of love that eases heartache.

The romantic in me could not have written a more beautiful or insane script than this relationship. I met a man by the sea where I once walked with my baby. A man who knows God, his own heart, and his dreams. A man who wishes to protect me. A man who, despite never knowing my daughter, always craves to hear more stories from those who loved her and keeps a picture of her on his nightstand. A man who now has a cardinal who visits him here in the States, and who whispered to me excitedly one day to look outside and see that there were now baby cardinals joining the male and female adult ones. Life and creation glowing right in front of us.

How does this relationship work? Well, how does love ever work? We're from two different countries and two different generations, and yet somehow it is the most seamless and nurturing relationship I've had my entire life. Committing to someone is never easy, but believe me, you will know when you are in a relationship that is not a struggle. I know what it is to plan and plot and pray your way into spaces that you hope you can make fit. And now suddenly, as I wander through the ashes, I have found someone strong enough to grab my hand and walk with me. Willing to navigate the land mines on my behalf. Wanting to help me find those new dreams and broaden the expanse of a horizon that seemed impossible to me just a year or two ago.

If my life has taught me one thing, it has taught me that nothing is for certain. Whether on the world stage or in our backyard, at some point we all get rocked to our core. Perhaps mine looks different than yours. However, realizing that your *before* is gone forever, and that you now have to find a new way, is something we all must do at some point in our lives. I never imagined loving again. I never imagined someone like Axel walking into my life. There are no guarantees. And yet—the universe dares us to try.

I have learned that instead of checking off boxes in your head, it is better to just stand still and listen to your heart. To listen to God. When you're not looking, when you're not trying, sometimes even when you can't imagine the possibility, God shows up. Hope shows up. Promise and laughter and love show up.

My great-grandma Lena used to say to "wear the world like a loose garment." I understand that in a profound way now. I am living in the moment every day and planning for the future while knowing the only certainty is uncertainty. There is a freedom in not being tied to the end of the story. As a writer, I always wrote backward from the end. Now I'm learning that we can only walk and write in a linear fashion, with each page and each chapter revealing itself only when it arrives. Our plans and story arcs can be altered or broken or shattered completely, but there are still pages. They may be blank or furiously scribbled over, but they are still waiting for the next word.

No, I can't guarantee what will happen with Axel. He can't promise me that we will spend the rest of our lives together. I can't promise him that either. But I can promise him today. Today, we walk hand in hand together. Today, we pray together. Today we laugh, we take care of each other, we listen to each other, and we protect each other. We plan and pray for a tomorrow that is unknown, but mostly we just focus on today. Because when I was looking for nothing more than peace and solitude on the sand where my baby walked, somehow, some way, tomorrow showed up.

— 27 —

Seek Joy

I found that there is a place . . .
"Down by the riverside" as the old folks used to sing.
It isn't easy to get to, but it's not far away . . .

You just have to look deep,
And dark,
And long,
And hard,
At your world.

In the mist of the cool waters,
In the midst of my life,

I
Found
Joy.

Not happiness . . . that fleeting child,
That ebbs and flows with the tide.
But the stuff that makes your spirit tingle
When you hear someone talk about going to hell . . .
And makin' it back.

THE OTHER SIDE OF YET

It comes when you can laugh from your gut,
Long after childlike wonder and innocence
Are stolen by life's tricks and betrayals.

When you get past the glass being half-full
Or half-empty . . .
'Cause most of us ain't got a glass at all.

So, you learn to cup your hands tightly to catch the cool drops,
And to gently part your fingers when it's time to let go.

I've watched the sun set in the wilderness of my soul,
And have rejoiced in the triumph of a new dawn.

I'm no longer spring's child . . .
Anticipating sunny days
And fearful of skies not blue.

I am the burning browns of autumn,
Facing the winter without hesitation,
'Cause I know the spring will come again

My great-grandma always said
"Wear the world like a loose garment"
I get it now.

As I walk on
"Down by the riverside,"
As the old folks still sing
I hold on loosely to the dashed dreams
And those realized,
The pain,
The happiness,
The tears,
The laughter,

Seek Joy

The lost loves,
The new hopes,

I
Found
Joy
And my soul looks back and wonders . . .
            —"Down By The Riverside" by Michelle Hord

While grief is ever present, remember that there is also a progression. It's so important to pay attention to your progress. It will be something to hold on to during the darker days. Early on, I was desperate to see my cardinal, crying whenever it would fly away. Months later, I would smile when it flew away, simply grateful for the visit. My faith has grown. My hope has been fortified. I know that whether it is a live cardinal in New York or the cardinal-themed chemo room where I sat with my dear sorority sister during her treatment, my baby is near. Her spirit is present. Friends still delight in sending me pictures of cardinals and butterflies. Carmen's youngest daughter now whispers, "Hi Gabrielle," whenever she sees a butterfly.

All of this took time and patience to embrace.

Grief and loss are like clay. They are malleable; a mass that can be physically held and felt. Grief in the hands of God can be smoothed and shaped into something brilliant. Yes, it requires a kiln where fire will burn off some stuff. And yes, it needs time—to cure. But in the *after* season, grief can shine because of and despite the fire making room for joy.

And what do we do in the meantime?

We hold on. We make room for joy.

There will be many *yets* we'll have to overcome in order to reach our *after* and reclaim our lives. As we have discussed in earlier chapters, there is a dichotomy in the healing process. There are pieces of your *before* you'll have to let go of, and yet there are pieces of your beliefs, your memories, your spirit that you have to somehow remember to pick up and take along.

THE OTHER SIDE OF YET

The first year after losing Gabrielle was filled with crushing firsts. Even if a day wasn't significant, "a year ago (or two, three) that or this day" always meant a time when Gabi Bear was alive and with me. Holidays, birthdays, anniversaries are all loaded bombs that feel strapped to my heart. With the slightest unintentional setback or move, these emotional land mines pull me back into the throes of my grief. I didn't sleep much at all that first year. In fact, I didn't even sleep much the second year. My morning rituals were my survival tactics. I held on desperately to everything—even things I didn't want—because I was fearful of losing anything else.

Sometime after the trial, something strange started to happen. I don't know if it was the universe, my clumsiness, or my subconscious, but I started losing things. I lost one of the earrings Hank gave me when Gabrielle was born. I hadn't worn them in so long because they felt like a searing reminder. One day one earring was just gone. Shortly after Gabrielle was murdered, a dear childhood friend, Denise, had a Wonder Woman–style bracelet made for me. On the inside, it said, "You are stronger than you know." I wore it religiously every day those first years. One day I felt my wrist and it was gone. On Axel's birthday, we went out on an ocean excursion and suddenly my sunglasses literally flew off my face and into the sea. Sunglasses that I had purchased as part of my "uniform" for the trial, as armor against strangers and the press. I was incredibly frustrated at the sudden losses of these things I saw as valuable, and Axel helped me look at it differently. "Maybe you didn't need them anymore. Maybe those things were just things and no longer serve the purpose they once served." It was then that I learned that if I was willing to "lose" some of the pain and weight I had held on to so desperately for years, I could find the space to seek and choose joy.

And now I know that it is okay to choose joy for myself. My *after* continues to be written every day. As I, physically and emotionally, move further away from the day-to-day trauma of my *before*, I operate in the world differently. I have a different confidence. I have a different life's work and priorities. I embrace each day of *after*, whether it's a day of smooth sailing or one of unforeseen continued legal challenges and expenses. This new life of mine is a falling golden leaf blown about by the wind. It floats around indiscriminately and in places I could have never imagined—but always with a marked beauty and a divine purpose. Trusting God with my *after* is the only way forward for me.

BUT HOW DO I hold on and choose joy through these progressions, Michelle?

It definitely is not easy. With every new place, space, and face, there are new emotions to reckon with. It's why I came up with an acronym that I use to remind myself and others of how to move through grief with grace. Through it all we must hold on to our S.P.I.R.I.T.

The first thing we have to do is SURVIVE. There will be times when it will just be about getting through the day. It's giving yourself mercy for small victories. Part of accepting your *after* and building your next chapter is accepting victory when and where you can find it and knowing that you will be able to fight another day no matter what. You have to reimagine success and retrofit your life into new shapes and measures. For me? Surviving has taken on many forms. Some days it was—and still is—staying in bed and ignoring the demands of the day. I have had to learn that I am allowed to slow down. I have had to learn to acknowledge my pain rather than push through it and to give myself space to fully sit in my grief. Even now. Other days, surviving means the exact opposite. It means pushing through. Crying in the shower but showing up fierce wherever I am supposed to be that day. Be graceful and gentle with yourself when you can and push yourself to keep going when you must. It is all surviving. All of it. It may look and feel different, and it certainly isn't a linear process, but as often said, keep breathing. Keep dancing. Keep going. Surviving is anything and everything except giving up. And even in the darkest moments we have opportunities to seek the light of joy.

Next, give PRAISE. Whether you are religious, spiritual, or not, we all have things to be grateful for. Find a way to actively acknowledge the good in your life; a way to notice when joy has arrived in your space and in your body. An attitude of gratitude has been a fundamental part of my defiant faith. As I struggled through my first holiday season, I was still grateful. Grateful that Gabrielle chose me to spend seven-plus years of her earthly voyage. Grateful for all of the pictures, presents, and memories with my little girl. Grateful to be able to meet other children who were in need of so much during my mission work and whose smiles lit up the dark spaces in my heart. Gratitude sparked my "Hallelujah anyhow!" In the middle of it all, be bold enough to stand in gratitude for what you do have; for what is left and what is to come.

Third, make an IMPACT. As much as we need them at times, it can eventually become claustrophobic in our cocoons. Find a way to look outside yourself. Get outside of yourself and your circumstances. Change your point of view and you can change how you cope. If you can't feel joy, it might mean accessing it in a way you never expected before.

The truth is, there is no greater satisfaction than stepping outside of yourself to serve others. In moments of darkness, when there's no semblance of perspective or ability to see outside of your own abyss, making an impact on other people's lives gives you a reprieve. When you reach out to others, the connection can save you both. That doesn't mean you have to start a nonprofit. You could make dinner for an elderly neighbor. You could pay for the next person's coffee in line at the coffee shop. You'll be surprised how offering even just a little bit of yourself in these ways can carry you through the dark days. These actions can become emblematic of your defiant faith. If you process nothing else I've written, know this: You must think outside of the box. The box is you and what you're facing. Get outside of it and smell the fresh air. Truly *see* the people around you and look for a way to make a difference for them. In turn, you will be telling the universe that you are not giving up. That you are still seeking the light. That you can still summon the will to make a difference.

Don't forget to take moments to REFLECT. When we are faced with seemingly insurmountable obstacles, it is so important to remember who we are. Life, labels, and strife can sometimes rip away the fundamental beliefs you have about yourself in the world. Look in the mirror. Open up your mental account of your life's journey and remind yourself of who you are and what you've already done in the world. Look back on your other battles without comparing pain. Examine the processes. Remember that relationship you never thought you'd get over? Remember that job you dreamed about but couldn't imagine doing? Remember that emotional and spiritual trek you made as you headed up a proverbial mountain? It was a steep and treacherous climb, right? But then suddenly, there you were, standing in the sunshine, at the top, able to see your way to the other side.

When you don't know how you'll get over, when you can't feel joy no matter how hard you try, look back, and marvel at what you've already done. Access past joys. Remember what that smile or that event felt like in your body. Remember when you overcame that last obstacle. And then use your awareness of those past joys and pains, along with your faith, as an insurance policy assuring that you still have what you need to survive. I found myself reflecting on losing my mother and grandmother in my twenties when I lost Gabrielle. I couldn't equate that past pain and grief with the present. But I did sense that whatever got me through then—however painful or ugly or insurmountable those mountains of loss and despair felt decades ago—might be the same resilience that I needed to reach for now. Look for times in your past when you have been brave, strong, or have overcome hardship. No matter how different those circumstances are from your present challenges, it is enormously helpful to reflect on your own survival muscles. You have gotten through hardship before—that means you can do it again.

Dare to IMAGINE a world where you have the power to create a new *after* for yourself. In times of scarcity, it is important to remember that you still have a future. None of us know what's next. The current state of our world has done a great job of reminding us of this very thing. But as long as the sun rises, there are new days to imagine; new ways to reinvent who you can be and create the life you want. A life filled not just with the temporary emotions of happiness or excitement, but with the joy that comes from within. The joy that exists without perfect circumstances. When you pivot from being a thermometer to being a thermostat, you empower yourself to make what you need when you need it.

In some ways this may be the most difficult task. There is nothing that seems crazier when you're in pain and in a pit of loss, when you are stuck trying to hold on to your *yet*, than to imagine your *after*. *What will life look like? Will there be love? Will there be things that make me happy? Will it ever make sense? Is it necessary that it does?*

Remember that the wreck has already happened. You have survived whether you wanted to or not. You cannot apologize for walking on land again. So now is the time to take the reflections of where you've been, the impact you may want to make in the world, your gratitude for all you've been given, your basic survival skills, and imagine a tomorrow. Probably one completely unlike what you previously thought would be your lot. Yes, your entire future landscape may seem completely foreign. But part of the battle is won in holding on to enough hope to try. It's actually not as important whether you actualize those dreams exactly. What is important is that you give yourself permission to dream and try. Faith and hope come in the attempt. At the boldness of saying, "I may not even want to go, but I'm going to imagine a future." Imagine a time when things will feel different than they do today. A time when an underlying satisfaction and joy are possible.

For all I've done and all the courage I have tried to muster in difficult moments, perhaps the boldest thing I've done so far is imagine a future. Pace yourself. Sure, at one point early on, I feared completely losing hope. In that moment, wanting hope was enough for me to make progress. Months after my daughter's murder? With no resolution on any front? The mere desire for hope was enough. Be kind to yourself. But push yourself too. What type of future can you imagine? Could success or love look different? Even if things will never be the way you dreamed, can you imagine another way to live?

Finally, TESTIFY every chance you get. Your test is the catalyst for your testimony, and it is yours to share. What story are you supposed to tell? How can you bear witness to moments of pain and triumph and share them? I don't necessarily mean shouting your pain from the rooftop or sharing on some great platform. It might not mean writing a book or a blog. It may not require you to grace a stage. You might be called to share your story with a friend who is struggling or touch the heart of a person you don't know. Do not bottle your experiences up; you must let them out. Sharing will help you better understand your story, and you will likely be surprised to find that you have more company on this road than you think.

Pardon the mash-up of my Baptist girl background and *Hamilton* show tunes, but as Lin-Manuel Miranda asks in the beloved musical: *Who will tell your story?* Who better than you? History really does have its eye on you. Maybe only in your house, school, church, or family, but your steps and choices at this point in your journey will absolutely write the story of who you are and how you choose to exist in this world. There have been so many moments while writing this book that I have stopped and shuddered and asked, "Why should I be telling my story? There are so many people with stories to tell." Then I remind myself that it isn't really about me. If I can testify, if I can tell my story, then my testimony just might save someone else. It may save someone from giving up, giving in, or tapping out. You never know when your story will turn into the very thing someone needs to make it through the day. One of the most powerful experiences for me in the past several years has been reading through the letters, emails, and texts from friends and strangers alike who said my faith made a difference for them. Maybe it brought someone back to their faith. Maybe it gave them permission to feel what they feel in totality. Maybe it gave them perspective where they'd had none. Maybe it gave them the guts to make a hard decision or be audacious enough to seek out joy. Whatever the outcome, know that being willing to share your testimony has an exponential impact.

Your story belongs to you, but your testimony may be more for someone else. Inspiration often comes from information, and vulnerability begets more vulnerability. Testifying allows us to find wide-open spaces where courageous choices are possible. It's in those spaces where we don't give up. Where we see our story through to the end. What's your testimony? Tell it. And not just the good stuff. Someone's life might depend on it.

CALL ME CRAZY, but I'm one of those people who doesn't mind getting lost. It could be because I have such a bad sense of direction, so it's my way of compensating for that fact. Whenever I would get lost with Gabrielle in the car, I would say to her, "We are on an adventure!" As she got older and savvier, she figured out my euphemism and would inevitably say, "Mommy, are you lost?" We were both right. Yes, I was probably lost. And yes, being lost had opened up the possibility to discover something new; an adventure.

The older I get, the more I realize how dangerous it is to keep score. How much do I make? What's my ideal weight? Why does it seem like other people have it easier than me? Why can't I find the right mate? How dare they say anything—they have been through nothing compared to me! This is a kind of oppression Olympics that will never satisfy you. It is a race you can never win. The numbers literally will never add up in a way that is productive or bring you peace or allow for vulnerability or intimacy.

Were there some inevitable factors of my former life? Sure. I had a child. She was going to grow up. I was going to have to change and morph to meet her development as she moved from baby to child to teen to adult. I would need to make a certain amount of money to ensure she could have the exposure I wanted for her and the freedom to go to any college she wanted. We kept an account of her height, weight, age, and grade. All of this, added together, *should* have equaled her living a long and fruitful life buoyed by the love of her parents. But now none of those numbers add up. In fact, the whole damn spreadsheet flew out of the window.

When you can't keep score or measure yourself against others, and when you realize you not only are unsure of the destination but are uncertain if you even have the right map to get you there, you are lost. *And* on an adventure. We will all get somewhere. We will all experience something. So toast the process. The most important thing you'll ever do is hold on to your S.P.I.R.I.T. and keep going. Mark your time only by breaths, love, laughter, and tears. At some point you'll look back and see that while it may have felt like you were marching in place, you've somehow made it down a new road. Where you are going will become less and less important than *how* you are moving, breathing, and persevering.

The common tendency is to equate emotional or psychological brokenness to a physical break or injury. But I believe heart healing is more art than science. We can't keep score, because it changes every day. We can't get on the emotional scale and find out we somehow worked off fifteen pain pounds like we were following some kind of diet fad. So instead, we must learn to toast the process. Accept ambiguity. Recognize that there will be victories and setbacks. Trust that you will survive and find reasons to be thankful for something every day. Find a way to lift someone else. Use your own experiences as inspiration for this current trek and tell it. Tell your story. Joy isn't some fly-by-night, uncontrollable emotion. It's not an inevitability either, like hunger or exhaustion. Joy is a choice. It is something that happens *despite* pain or loss or struggle. It is the audacity of a gut laugh in the dark. It is the warmth of love or the excitement of new possibilities in the midst of it all. It is the defiance to go for it. Whatever *it* is. It's the decision to indulge our desires. To be impractical. To ignore the odds and skip to the ending. I've had to choose joy every single day. I've had to come to terms and be at peace with this healing journey enough to make space for joy. Things that can float by without recognition when you live in the cloudiness of your circumstances can pop out and offer moments of delight if you let them. A great meal. An easy conversation with an old friend. The beauty of a silent snowfall. A burst of red in a rose, or in a cardinal. Embrace the beauty in those little miracles. Express your gratitude for grace. Keep choosing joy each day not because of where you are but in spite of where you've been.

— 28 —

Lean in to Change

December 26, 2020
Life is a series of seasons. I am blessed to start a new one now.
Saying goodbye (temporarily) to the frozen Big Apple with a final
moment at Gabrielle's Playground.

Next stop?

My second home in the Bahamas with my now fiancé, Axel.

A new spring is dawning even in the darkest days of the year.
Perhaps I will never completely heal, yet I still have another
chance to once again be whole.

In the third year after the trial, things changed. I wrestled with sharing my new relationship with Axel with the others in my life. I was afraid that people would misunderstand it as a "moving on." They'd wrongly believe that I was "well" or it was "over." Deep down, though, I knew that no one who loves me has ever made that mistake. It was more about how I felt. In the same way that I refused to wear makeup for so long to try to externally reflect the bleakness I felt inside, I feared any good or happiness would somehow give people the wrong impression. I am moving forward, but never without Gabrielle. It has been difficult at times to reconcile with making new choices and creating a new life, because I was so afraid that the world would think I was "better" and because I didn't want to ever appear as if I was leaving Gabrielle behind.

Yet, I know what Gabrielle would want for her mommy. It is the same thing I want for you. To go for it. Whatever *it* is for you. Whatever brings goodness and peace and joy into your life. The same courage that has helped you tackle the pain or loss or disillusionment of your *before*, and gave you the strength to proclaim a *yet*, will also propel you into your *after*. Lean in to the change. Know that it is a part of the healing process and that you can move on without moving away from things in your *before* that matter to you the most.

My life and lifestyle have definitely changed. I have taken professional and personal risks as a result of this journey. When I went back to work in late August, after Gabrielle was murdered, I was blessed to work for Cara Stein, a woman who was very loving and supportive. That made all the difference at the time. She'd shared with me her story of having breast cancer, and before she went back to work, after having her surgeries and chemo, she had her direct reports come to see her one at a time at her house. She suggested that it might be a good option for my team and me to do as well. I thought it was a brilliant idea. One at a time, from all over the country, my direct reports would come to the house and sit with me. We'd sit and cry together and have our moment. Then we would start talking about work to get me acclimated. That was such great preparation, I think, on both sides. It gave us all a place to put our feelings about our personal relationships before we pivoted back into a professional dynamic.

On my first official day back, I had my monthly all-team meeting with my eighty-plus reports from five different locations. It looked like the *Star Trek Enterprise* with all the screens. When I walked back into the office that first day, I was shaking. I was in a cold sweat. I had Barbara in my purse, and I went and sat down in Cara's office and just started crying. I said, "I don't know if I'm ready for this." And Cara said, "Take it at your own pace."

I remember feeling like I was walking in slow motion as I made my way through the hallways, knowing the last time I'd walked in these hallways, my life was a completely different life. The last time I'd been in Cara's office was right before I left to sign the divorce papers, and I had told her excitedly, "He's agreed to sign." And she smiled and said, "I think things are really going to turn around for you now." And so to retrace those steps in this new heart space felt like when you go back to high school and the lockers all look small. Everything to me just looked like I was Alice in Wonderland—a different dimension. When I got to the teleconference room for the meeting with the team, I was trying not to cry. But I opened up with "The last time I sat here with all of you, my life was completely different. And almost everything I thought I knew is gone except for you." My voice broke a little bit when I said that last part. I continued, "This team is still a team. You're still here and I'm still here too." The love and support across those many two-dimensional screens was 3D and palpable.

Taking the risk to be vulnerable made returning to work better, but it also revealed to me the different direction my life was going.

After the trial, I decided that I was ready to turn the page on almost three decades of working in corporate America at various media outlets. I had been to hell and back. I literally had nothing to lose. So I decided to bet on myself. It wasn't a decision made lightly or without plans or thoughts. But I decided to step out on that defiant faith that had served me so well through pain and turn it toward my possibility. I decided to share my story and hopefully help others. I walked away from many things professionally perhaps, but in my new *after* life of writing and media consulting, I am finding a richness of experiences that has given me so much more.

It took me a while, but I eventually learned that I didn't have to choose between my grief and my joy. They will forever live side by side. My brother, Noel, wisely said to me once, as I sat on a balcony watching the waves of the ocean, "Both can be true, Michelle. You can find joy and love and peace and still hold all of the love and pain and memories for Gabrielle. All at once."

A few months ago Axel looked at me and smiled.

"What is it?" I asked, returning his grin.

"You don't have those dark circles under your eyes anymore. You sleep better now, and it shows."

My initial internal reflex was to be offended. Was he suggesting I was over it? But I quickly realized that's not what he was saying at all. He was simply acknowledging the evidence of this new season in my life. He is an attentive man and was celebrating my victories, in the same way he has helped me manage the defeats.

During the COVID pandemic, I decided to start a book club in Gabrielle's memory, as a part of my foundation, Gabrielle's Wings. It's called Gabrielle's Book Club, and it's a great way to introduce children to books from around the world and to connect each child with others—especially during the time of remote learning. Because exposing children to diverse images through reading is a cornerstone of the work we do at Gabrielle's Wings, we have established learning nooks/centers around the globe called "Gabrielle's Corners."

We launched the book club with a book called *Amazing Grace* by Mary Hoffman, which I must have read to Gabrielle a million times. The day before and day of the launch event I felt sick. Worse than I'd felt all year. My asthma flared and I was having difficulty breathing. That morning, I cried. Grief had shown up in my body again. I grabbed Gabrielle's copy of the book and read it for the first time since I'd last read it to her. Since she'd last crawled into my lap, long legs and all, and listened to my voice soothe her into sleep. Reading it this time, I realized that I was afraid. I was afraid of getting upset in front of the children participating. I was afraid that someone would ask me a question I was unprepared for.

At one point in the afternoon, I finally broke down. Axel held me and said, "You've suffered so much, and then you go out and put on a brave face for those kids. Afterwards you are left to be alone with your pain. Or, you used to be alone. Now I am here." My relationship with Axel is also part of this grief progression. There's something about knowing that you are loved. There's something powerful about having someone who knows when and how I sleep; when and why I'm worried; when I last ate or exercised. There's something absolutely grounding about having someone waiting on the other side of the lectern or Zoom call who can meet my eyes and see past what the public sees. Despite the solitary grief that my loss often has brought, I have also been blessed to have eyes to lock with as I talk about Gabrielle, honor her memory, try to do work in her name. There is a hand, a shoulder, a quiet voice, that has always been close when I needed it in the darkness.

Creating a new life for yourself is all a process. I went from being unable to even look through Gabrielle's things to working with Axel and an organizer to make hard decisions about what to keep and what to let go. I have somewhat adopted Gabrielle's former nanny, Flor, and her three-year-old son. He has Gabrielle's favorite stuffed giraffe among other things of hers now. As the fourth holiday season without Gabrielle approaches, I've finally been able to offer Flor many of my holiday decorations. All of the organized boxes of decorations, for every holiday under the sun, can now bring joy to her and her little one. No, I may not be able to celebrate in that way right now, but I'm finally okay with sharing the things that once brought me so much joy with others.

Much like the pencil marks in Gabrielle's room that marked her growth over the years, change and progression happen slowly. Sometimes you don't see the changes that are happening, and you need someone else to help you step back to see the progress. It doesn't happen every night, but now I can sleep. It doesn't happen with every event, but now I have someone to turn to when the weight of my work with children becomes too triggering. I can see the changes in myself through the hopeful eyes of those who love me, and it reminds me to step back and appreciate the growth that is taking place within me.

"We need him to love you like we do, and I think he might," said Wanda, one of the Five, when I shared my engagement news. Here was a conversation with a dear friend who had once worried about scheduling someone to spend the night with me in the first months and years, so that I would never be alone. A conversation that I am sure she and the Five probably prayed for, but that was inconceivable to me for so long.

To be clear: You do not need a new partner to progress. I am grateful for my relationship with Axel, but my journey and victory are not contingent on his presence. My lesson, my growth, is found in our today and what it took for me to get here. A huge point of progression for me was to not only trust love enough to hold on to someone new, but to have the faith that I can let go and survive, if I must. In fact, I think the only way to truly embrace new love as part of change is to know that a new stronger self-love must always come first.

And remember, life is not linear. We don't live a singular *before*, then a singular *yet*, and then a singular *after*. Remember our hero's journey? It is a continuum. Yes, there are some profound moments of change in your life that are never repeated or rivaled. However, we have the power to reinvent our choices and create new change and possibility in our lives always. Whether we create our own change or are reeling from an unexpected or unwanted change, change will come. Keep that defiant faith. Hold on to that warrior of hope's spirit. Life offers a series of *yet* opportunities and *yet* moments, if we are only brave enough to keep looking for new light and brighter new dawns.

— 29 —
Survive Through Serving Others

Someone saw in me a gift. They loved me as though I was their own. Let me see the world was bigger than NE Deanwood, DC. Tucked me in at night. Woke me up with the words "Good Morning, Sunshine!" Let me order pigs in a blanket and assured me it was better than McDonald's. Let me see Broadway plays rather than movie theaters. Taught me how to eat at five-star restaurants. Made sure I was fed and had money to travel to school. Helped me with homework and had all her friends whom I consider Aunties and Uncles to help as well. Shared her family with me that became my family. Told me "Excuses were tools of the incompetent, building bridges to nowhere, monuments to nothing." Sent me to prom. And always I LOVE YOU. Gave me the eyes like a mother, warmed my hands in the cold. The list goes on. This is dedicated to my sister Michelle Hord-White. And even in my adult years, she still holds my hand with love and prayer. Never giving up on me. I love you, Big Sis!
                              —Facebook post from Neta Vaught

I grew up the granddaughter of a Baptist minister and the daughter of parents who created a nonprofit dedicated to helping Black students achieve their goals of higher education. The Hord Foundation is more than twenty-five years old and has raised millions of dollars. "Service is the rent we pay" is something I heard often growing up. When I lost Gabrielle, people immediately wanted some kind of call to action, and when I asked them to donate to my parents' foundation, the response was overwhelming. That first gift, a new kitchen for Gabrielle's Girl Scout house, filled my heart with so much joy. Later, watching children squeal in delight on the playground named after her did the same. Traveling to South Africa to see children wearing bracelets with her name, who now know that a child who looks like them "gifted" them books and computer supplies, nearly made my soul burst. But this wasn't my first time realizing that service was a way toward healing. That understanding came many years before. Yes, it certainly was in my genes to be of service, but it was in my early adulthood that I learned the most powerful part of service was beyond obligatory. There was salvation in the service. I found that whatever I was doing for others, whatever enrichment I was giving others, it was also giving me fuel to go on when I felt like I was on fumes.

Once I'd graduated from college, got a job, and had a year or two under my belt, I felt compelled to find a way to serve again. I'd obviously heard about the Big Brothers, Big Sisters program, and had always enjoyed being a mentor. So I went to an open call for Big Sisters in Washington, DC. While driving to the meeting, I spoke with my mom, saying, "I'm going to this thing tonight. I don't know if I have time. With this job, I can be put on a plane and have to crash a piece at any time. I'm working around the clock and I don't have any money. I'm going to go, but I don't think I'll wind up doing it." Nevertheless, I went, sat there, and listened to the presentation.

I was certainly moved by what being a Big Sister could mean. I was more moved by the fact that I was the only brown person in the audience. I knew that the majority of the girls we were talking about would look like me, and that triggered something inside. I was blessed to have had role models in my house, my family, and my lineage. But there are many children who don't have that for whatever reason. I knew it was important for these girls to not just have a mentor but for that mentor to be someone who looked like them. Someone they could truly see themselves in. They needed to know that salvation could look like me too.

So when I realized that I was the only Black woman there, and I listened to these very well-meaning women who had very clear parameters about where they were willing to travel, what neighborhoods they were comfortable going to, I saw clearly the impact that I could make. So partly with my Howard University *Fight the Power* stance still fresh on my back, and a bit of my rebel attitude, at the end I went up to the woman giving the presentation and said, "Give me a girl who you haven't been able to place." That's when she told me a story about Neta. For whatever reason, the Big Sisters she'd been assigned in the past had fallen through a few times.

I'll never forget pulling up to the apartment that first day, and this beautiful little girl with these big brown eyes was sitting in the window waiting for me. My heart just melted. I went inside and met her family. I took her to the Pentagon City Mall for our first outing, because that's just what you did in the nineties! Her grandmother had given her a few dollars to take with her, which told me so much about the family she came from: No matter their trials, whatever they may or may not have had, they made sure this little girl wasn't walking through the door empty-handed. But what moved my heart even more was that Neta used her money not to buy a toy or trinket for herself, but to buy *me* a little Thumper key chain from the Disney Store. This eleven-year-old girl taught me something about gratitude that day and I was all in.

After I left Neta's house that first day, I called my mom and said, "Oh, Mom, this little girl, she's already stolen my heart. I'm so grateful I'm doing this. I know it's going to be hard but I'm so glad I moved forward." She was very happy for me. A month later, Mom died, and serving Neta, being there for her, watching this brilliant little girl navigate such hard circumstances, was a kind of salvation for me.

This isn't a Lifetime movie, so there isn't some nice and neat ending to the story. When I talk about salvation, it's not about being someone's savior. It's more about serving each other's hearts through relationship and growing together. Neta's life didn't magically get better because I entered it. She had ups and downs. But the beauty of it all is she's a fighter. She continues to fight. All of her kids are on scholarships in private schools. She's doing her best and that's what matters.

Now I often think about how powerful it was that God chose to put me in this maternal capacity just as I was losing my mother and grandmother. Today I think about being not only a motherless daughter, but a daughterless mother. It's why I've chosen to take in other daughters; to be what I had wanted to be for Gabrielle. I get to be a model for other children who look like Gabrielle, but do not necessarily have the privileges or exposure she had. And to not only give them those things, but for them to know that the source of those things is someone who looks just like them. I didn't know it back in 1994 when I met Neta, but I think the seed of Gabrielle's Wings was planted then.

Service is the secret to my survival, whether I was being a Big Sister or planning to give my first donation to Gabrielle's Girl Scout house on what would have been her eighth birthday. Based on my experiences when I was younger, I know that the only way forward, the only way out, is to try to fight for the light. And if there isn't any I can see, I'm going to light a freaking match—my service—in the dark.

Gabrielle's Wings is another match I've lit to light the dark.

After my mom died, there was always this juxtaposition of the anniversary of her death and literally within two weeks our annual event fundraiser for the Hord Foundation, which really had become like a memorial to her. So within the first day or two of losing Gabrielle, someone came to me and said, "Listen, people want to do something. They want to raise money." I said, "Well, tell whoever's asking to give money to the Hord Foundation." Within six weeks we'd raised $150,000.

At that point, I realized that maybe I needed to create a separate entity. I love the work that the Hord Foundation does, but it is focused solely on college scholarships for children of color from Connecticut. Gabrielle wasn't a high school student. She didn't get that far. And so what started to feel more appropriate for me—and my family's foundation and board were generous enough to work with me in the early months when I was grappling with this—was to figure out how to serve younger children and create a different mission.

I'd created an acronym out of our last name for the Hord Foundation: Helping Others Realize their Dreams. And so I wanted to do the same thing for the work we did for young kids. After that first gift for the Girl Scout kitchen, we built our first Gabrielle's Corner at the local library with books about kindness and inclusion. Then I went on my first missionary trip with Believers' World Outreach, which opened my eyes to the broader opportunities to help children of color. It was a slow build, but I emailed my village in probably November or December of 2017 saying, "I've got to come up with a name. We need to be our own thing." And my friend Katie suggested Gabrielle's Wings: "I love it because it makes me think of her little angel wings. You also talk about her loving butterflies. And if you put it all together, it's also Gabrielle swings, which makes me think of her being really playful." I fell in love with it.

I officially announced Gabrielle's Wings at our family gala the following February. While it's been logistically challenging to break away from my family foundation, it has absolutely been worth it. I remember meeting with a tax attorney to talk it all through. He said, in a very straightforward but powerful way, "You need to take some time to decide whether this was therapy or something you really want to do." And that was absolutely the right thing to consider.

I did exactly that. I took that first year and made all contributions through the Hord Foundation. But I finally arrived at the decision that this was more than just a way to work through grief. It was also a purpose. A path. I realized that this was my balm in Gilead. Yes, this was going to be the thing, when I was having a bad day, that I could hold on to tightly. I can go through pictures from the building of the playground architecture and remember standing up in front of the moist eyes of children and parents. But this is also the creation of Gabrielle's legacy.

When I went to Cape Town and walked into the portable trailer where Gabrielle's Corner sits and those little kids realized that I was Gabrielle's mom, the feeling was indescribable. These babies knew that Gabrielle was an angel who wanted them to have nice computers and books. These tiny, beautiful children have their little pictures of my Gabi Bear on buttons and little pink "We Love Gabrielle" elastic bands on their wrists. It moves me every time.

So eventually, as you serve your way through your grief, you may have to come to a point where you decide what that service will be for the long term. I had to pivot and figure out what I wanted Gabrielle's Wings to be. Because it couldn't just be a memorial to Gabrielle. It had to be bigger. It had to be about building a legacy, and so part of the letting go at that stage was moving from acting out of pure grief and into a space of celebrating her life and creating long-term impact. For Gabrielle's Wings to really soar, I had to get off the ground. I had to be brave enough to make it something bigger, and I had to ensure the story wasn't about me. To not make it about my loss, but to make it about the children we're helping and the positive changes we're making.

Yes, service will help you survive. But in the long run, there can be more. The legacy of what you lost can live on.

— 30 —

Plant Seeds for Your *After*

Do not fear, for I have redeemed you;
I have summoned you by name; you are mine.
When you pass through the waters,
I will be with you;
and when you pass through the rivers,
they will not sweep over you.
When you walk through the fire,
you will not be burned;
the flames will not set you ablaze.
—Isaiah 43:1b-2

Your life is not a memorial.

Some wounds don't heal, they scar. More than an impression, they leave imprints on your body and soul. The way we transition from our *yet* to our *after* is simple but not easy: We realize how much power we still have. We learn that, like Dorothy in *The Wizard of Oz*, everything you ever needed, you've had all along. Even when things you thought you couldn't survive without are no longer present, you have everything you need. No matter how many times you have to pivot from your past to your present, there will always be, as Isaiah also says, "beauty for your ashes." If you are willing to face your *before*, accept your *yet*, and learn to let go so you can open yourself up to love, joy, and peace again, you can surely walk through the fire, and the flames will not set you ablaze.

My brother, Noel, and I are incredibly close. We have a sibling shorthand drawn from childhood memories and shared experiences. We both loved the movie *Forrest Gump*. It came out the year our mom died and was one of the first movies I saw afterward. Noel and I have many lines committed to memory.

Lieutenant Dan is a supporting character in the film, a man who comes from a long line of US soldiers who fought and died in wars as far back as the Revolutionary War at the founding of the country. However, during his stint in the military, Dan didn't die on the battlefield as he believed was his birthright and legacy. Forrest Gump, the protagonist, saved his life. Forrest picked up Lieutenant Dan, blown to bits with no legs, and carried him to safety. For years, Lieutenant Dan wrestled with this. He ranted constantly about how his birthright was stolen from him. He referred to himself in the past tense. As if the old Dan had died back in that war.

"I *was* Lieutenant Dan!"

"You still *are* Lieutenant Dan," Forrest reminds him with childlike curiosity and confusion.

There it is.

The traumas that come into our lives can feel a lot like that war Forrest and Dan fought in. And there are too often moments when it feels like pieces of our bodies are gone. Like somehow everything we identified as part of our identity, as what made us who we are, has been violently blown away. After the murder of my Gabrielle, this is exactly how I felt. But that brother of mine said something to me one day that felt like a hint of promise even if I thought it was impossible. He said, "You still *are* Lieutenant Dan."

Something clicked.

I finally got it.

Noel was right.

It is critical that you also understand this about yourself and about this grief you carry. Even when I didn't want to be, even when it hurt, I was still Michelle. Broken. Devastated. Undone. But still Michelle.

And no matter what has happened, no matter how you've been hurt, you are still you. Different, but you. And armed with that knowledge, you have the power to take what is left of the *before* you, refine it in your *yet*, and graft it into your *after*.

THE COVID-19 CRISIS created new and awkward norms for us all. Whether it was the fear of hugging or gathering with loved ones, the difficulty speaking or hearing others in public through masks, or the fatigue of connecting via computer screens versus real-life human encounters, everyone seemed to be grappling with what it meant to live and love in this new reality.

This was particularly challenging for Gabrielle's Wings. Up until the pandemic, we'd focused heavily on creating collective experiences that helped educate, entertain, and enlighten youth. It was heartbreaking to drive past the beautiful playground with Gabrielle's name on it and see the yellow tape surrounding it. As a precaution, playgrounds were closed to try to stem the rate and spread of the virus.

Because I chose to scatter Gabrielle's ashes over the ocean she loved so much, her playground became a sanctuary and sacred place for me—a destination to go when I wanted to be alone with my little girl and my vast memories. I often enjoyed standing back or sitting in my car and watching strangers and their children play in the space, knowing that they were able to just enjoy it at face value.

It was a particularly crisp autumn day. The type of day that makes you think of football games and the smell of apple cider donuts; the crunch of golden leaves under your feet. It had been a week or so since I had driven past the playground, and so this morning, with coffee and a bagel, I decided to make the stop. Much to my surprise and delight, there were children there. There was no longer any yellow tape, and instead there was a family with two girls playing on the playground. It could have been a scene from any other time I'd visited before the pandemic, with the glaring exception of the masks both girls were wearing as they frolicked across monkey bars and slides. They excitedly watched brightly colored butterfly pinwheels spin magically in the wind above their heads.

I did not realize how much it would mean to me to see children playing on the playground once again until I arrived. I got out of my car and started walking toward the family. I'm always careful about approaching because I know how cautious I would have been to see an adult with no children watching my baby play. As I went to introduce myself to the father, he stopped me.

"We know who you are. You may not remember, but we met you here once before. How are you doing?"

The genuine compassion in his eyes felt like lead in my heart. They knew. They knew that their daughters were playing on a playground that was built out of pain and tears for another person's child. At one point, the father stopped the older daughter long enough to have her introduce herself to me. She looked to be not much younger than Gabrielle was when she died. She told me her name and then asked me mine. There's nothing I love more than an assertive and confident little girl! I asked her what her favorite part of the playground was, and as she stood there trying to be obedient talking to me, I could see her fidgeting. I shifted gears.

"Why don't you show me your favorite part instead?" I suggested.

A smile crept across her face and she skipped off to the monkey bars. Remaining on the perimeter of the playground, I took a couple of discreet pictures, mindful to not show the faces of the children who played there. I took a picture of the weeping cherry blossom tree that Gabrielle's Girl Scout troop had planted in her memory three years prior. This little tree had withstood two winters thus far and was preparing itself for the third. As I watched streams of brilliant sun hit the bright primary colors on the playground and listened to the squeals of delight from the two sisters, a monarch butterfly showed up. As often happens, it stayed for a while and circled as if to ensure that I saw it and knew that it was in fact for me.

"Thank you for the playground!" the little girl shouted as I was leaving and heading back to the car. Maybe the statement was an act of obedience nudged on by her parents. Maybe it was her own little heart filled with gratitude.

As I journey further into my *after*, I leave behind that ship from *before*. I leave it wrecked against the rocks of *before*, no longer recogniz-able. I relish small victories that are defined in inches and moments. In fact, I have redefined what a victory is altogether. Victory on that day at the playground was simply being brave enough to show up. It was then being brave enough to stay when I saw the family. It was being brave enough to engage with them and to tell them my story. And finally, victory was being brave enough to find joy in the delight of the children while also sitting in the middle of my sorrow for my own child. In my *before*, victory was measured in titles and promotions and my daughter's good grades and Girl Scout cookie sales. Today, victory is measured in my ability to smile at a little girl and genuinely delight in her reflection as it bounces against the golden backdrop of my little girl's memorial.

These small victories are part of that "Hallelujah anyhow" praise I learned about in the Black Baptist churches of my childhood. Some-times as we sojourn, we will be called to push forward into our next chapters, and in that daring, we discover not just a defiant faith, but a defiant praise. We discover a defiant joy. Perhaps even a defiant laugh that happens while tears roll down our faces. Commend yourself. This is not easy. However, the ability to take the weight and pain of your *before* and somehow carry it on your back, to put it in compact luggage so it fits in the overhead compartment of your life, is the *real* destination on this journey. Finding a way to carry it with you does not diminish the story or suggest you are "better." It just means you are able to begin again. It is a moment of gratitude for the sun even on a cold day. It is you standing in an assurance that what you carry with you won't break you. You may stumble, but you can keep going. It sometimes gets heavy, but that defiant praise says thanks to God, the universe, and your own spirit that you will keep on keeping on.

I HAVE A brown thumb. Literally, and most definitely in the plant realm. Across every era of my life, I have traditionally been the Grim Reaper of all things botanical and leafy. Gabrielle, on the other hand, was really good with plants. She enjoyed gardening and loved the science behind what it took to help something grow. We would hit the farmers' markets together in the spring and summer to see the fresh bounty, and she would eat whole tomatoes or cucumbers like they were apples.

On Mother's Day weekend 2017, Gabrielle came in the door from school on a Friday with a backpack filled with elementary school trinkets and gifts for Mother's Day. With a huge grin she pulled out a brown paper bag. When she opened it, her eyes went wide and she screamed, "I ruined it!" Inside the bag was a little plastic pot that had been turned upside down and was sitting atop a pile of soil with tiny seeds in it. I assured Gabrielle as she looked up at me with her big brown eyes filled with tears that the seeds would be fine. With a mother's determination to protect her baby's gift, I worked to turn the planter upright and ensured every little bit of soil was back inside. We wanted to make sure this pile of dirt had a chance to blossom.

That same day, Gabrielle also brought home a small silk bouquet of roses. "I like the pretend ones better," I remember her saying. "They last forever." That silk bouquet sits in a vase now like it has every day since she handed it to me.

But even more precious to me is the fact that the plant she gave me has also survived. Despite being tossed about and jumbled. Gabrielle only lived to see a little sprout push up through the dirt. We would check it out every morning in delight to see if it had made any progress overnight, not realizing that she had only a few weeks left to watch its growth.

After she died, this plant became incredibly dear and important to me. There is very little from my *before* to physically hold on to. There's Barbara, of course. But as far as living things that can still grow, there was only her last Mother's Day gift to me. I watched with bated breath as the sprout became a vine or two. As it continued to grow and was potted and repotted, I took a snapshot of it to send to her second-grade teachers; the ones who'd provided the seeds. I was hoping to find out what kind of plant it was in order to ensure it was cared for properly. One teacher responded saying they had no idea!

"Those little bags of dirt don't typically last much longer than the goldfish at the carnival," she said.

Not Gabrielle's plant, though. It was the little plant that could.

When I had to travel extensively for business, Gabrielle's former nanny, Flor, "plant sat" for me. She too was amazed at how through several moves, clumsy hands, and no clear sense of the type of plant, it somehow still thrived. It was not only alive, but the beauty of the plant would often stop people in their tracks. In fact, Flor had a hyperactive dog in her house once, and when it headed toward the plant, she panicked. But somehow that plant calmed the dog down. It was as if he sensed her reverence for it.

One day, I walked past the plant and did a double take. The tiny white flowers that moved between the leaves were changing, and out of them had popped little red peppers that were so bright they looked like toys. When friends stopped by, they joined me in praising the little miracle. So much lost in the past few years, and yet, new things were somehow still growing.

One day, almost three years after losing Gabrielle, I was walking hand in hand with Axel through a farmers' market in the Bahamas. I'd shared with him how much Gabrielle and I had enjoyed these market outings back in New York, and suddenly I was stopped in my tracks. There it was. The little tree with the almost-too-red peppers. I pulled out my phone excitedly to confirm the match with a picture of my plant back at home. It was a cayenne pepper plant! It was mostly perennial in its native habitat of subtropical and tropical regions. Isn't that just the way? I had to cross an ocean—to my beloved second home, the Bahamas, the place of dreams with Gabrielle—to name it. And just like my Gabrielle, the plant ended up being a bit spicy, colorful, and a lover of the sun.

When Axel and I returned to New York, he took great care of Gabrielle's plant. He comes from a family of farmers and knew what to do. He was gentle with it, talking to "Little Momma," as we'd named it in Gabrielle's honor. At one point, it started to look like the plant was dying. I felt desperate. I couldn't lose her plant. The last living thing remaining from her orbit. In that moment, I just couldn't lose one more thing.

As tears came to my eyes, Axel reassured me by breaking open one of the spicy peppers. There, right in front of me, were seeds. Beautiful, good seeds. If we wanted, this thing we were nurturing could bear fruit.

With Axel's careful hands and despite my anxious overwatering, Little Momma is still growing. At times, the leaves will yellow. Some will become brittle and fall to the earth. It will at times appear as if there is too much dried out and dead for the green living parts to survive. And yet, it is still here. Pruned. Changed. Marked. Growing. In the same pot, this plant bears fruit and sheds its dying parts all at the same time. It is the quintessential metaphor for how I have felt at times on this journey. Moving forward. Making decisions. Taking risks. Pruning for new growth and shedding things that can no longer travel with me. It felt so symbolic that Gabrielle's final Mother's Day gift would hold such a sustaining message.

We have begun to give seeds to loved ones so Little Momma can spread her leaves and love in other homes. We recently noticed a new small plant pushing its way through the dirt. A sprout that looked nothing like the cayenne pepper plant. Fortunately, I now know "there's an app for that," so I snapped a picture of it to discover what it was. It is called the tree of heaven and can grow rapidly while withstanding different climates and conditions. It is sometimes considered a nuisance and despite best efforts to contain it or rip it from its roots, it will keep coming back with a vengeance. The tree of heaven is also the visual centerpiece from the classic book *A Tree Grows in Brooklyn*, where it symbolized the grit of green that, in its own act of defiant faith, can push through concrete.

We know about pushing through, don't we?

I will eventually have to separate the two plants. In the meantime, the evolving cayenne pepper tree, tall and transformed, offers us both signs of loss and signs of new life. And the tree of heaven, just inches tall now, models for us what it means to fight against the odds, against the conditions, against whatever may come to destroy it, in its quest to stretch from the earth toward the sky.

Our journeys of love and loss and life have many seasons, my friend.

You may feel like part of you is that bold red pepper and part of you is the wilting and fading leaves all at the same time. That is okay. Acknowledge the loss but celebrate the signs of life. If you push through, you will discover that your defiant faith can work as a fertilizer. And like the life that sprouts now from my little tree of heaven, you can still rise from the earth regardless of what tries to destroy you.

Your confidence, your hope, your courage to dream new dreams and your guts to go for them, may look more like a volatile stock market graph than a skyrocketing arrow. But resilience is not about being strong nonstop. It is just about *not stopping*. Despite the obstacles. Despite the unknown. Despite the setbacks. Keep planting. Keep growing. And if you find at some point something you planned for, dreamed of, or loved can no longer be, know that you hold in your hands those seeds of hope. Plant them. Nurture them. Yet, there will still be more to come.

One day my soul just opened up
so the "God of my weary tears and years"
became the author of my thanksgiving and praise

One day my soul just opened up
and my ears perked up to the sound of a thumpin' bass
that wound up being the beat of my heart

One day my soul just opened up
and dawn no longer was a question but a promise
Love no longer was a hope but my healing
Life no longer was a journey just footsteps and moments of joy

One day my soul just opened up
and I learned the new math where
love isn't a lesser than or greater than, but an equal to

One day my soul just opened up
and the murky, misty gray dissolved into deep blues and passionate
  pinks,
you know, colors you have to feel

One day my soul just opened up
and what I once understood as friendship,
once understood as comfort,
once understood as easy, turned clearly into love

'Cause one day, baby, my soul just opened up
and I heard Etta's hallelujah chorus "At Last"
and I realized finally that you could lead me home
　　　　—"One Day My Soul Just Opened Up" by Michelle Hord

I got it all and lost it all. I had a map that was leading me to a place I will now never see. My life now is in permanent "rerouting" mode. And maybe that's the way things are supposed to be for my particular journey. I often don't know where I am going now, and sometimes I am so exhausted by the trip that I lose track of the miles on the road. But I am still rolling. I am looking for whatever caution signs life does offer. I am sometimes lost and yet it is all an adventure. I am toasting the process and acknowledging that I can be whole even if I am never completely healed. I am embracing my ability to find new ways to fashion together a life. There are pieces in my *after* that would have never fit my *before* puzzle. Yet, today, that is where my power lies. These new pieces can be wedged in enough to create a portrait and perhaps even let some light in through the cracks. Healed? Maybe not. Maybe never. Changed? Strengthened? Grateful? Loved? Filled to every edge of my being with life and hope? Yes.

As your GPS would say: You Are Here. But the beauty and adventurous challenge of this dance of life is that the songs keep changing. You keep on dancing. There are always new moves. There are always new roads to discover. Some maps are marked with bumps and dangerous curves, and some detours show up unexpectedly. So the challenge is to know that our destination isn't a specific place. Creating new life and new experiences for yourself allows you to always harness the power of *yet*. The power to change course. The power to create something new. With a defiant faith and a sojourner's heart, you will find that life is never static, and you can harness that hope warrior spirit to stay the course in your ongoing journey from your *before* to your *after* life.

Acknowledgments

I have written my whole life and I have always dreamed of writing a book. This is not a book I could have ever imagined writing because this is not a story one could ever imagine holding. Yet, it is now my story. This book is a testimony that I hope helps other people with their own tests. I am grateful to so many who have offered me love, support, and prayers throughout this journey.

First and foremost, I am grateful for a defiant faith that is proven real every day by God's amazing grace and mercy.

To my father, Noel Hord, who has acted as my coach, advisor, and cheerleader since my birth, thank you for your unwavering love and support. To my baby brother, Noel Daniel, we have walked together through life's triumphs and tragedies, developed our own language (literally), and have a shorthand that requires few words. Even in those moments where it must have felt impossible to know what to do, you both showed up . . . and that is more than most would have had the fortitude to bear. As Gabrielle would say to her Papa and Uncle Noel, "I love you soooooooooo much."

I come from a family with a rich tradition of spirituality, community service, and creativity. To the Hords, Ritchies, Grahams, and Tylers who make up my DNA and the "family" who have filled my life with so much encouragement and support, thank you. I am forever indebted to my genetic and adopted aunts, uncles, and cousins who have stood in the gaps that life created for me and offered unwavering love and support across the years and miles. To the writers in my family, who quizzed me on summer reading and asked me to share my work out loud: Aunt Katherine, Uncle Fred, Uncle Kenny, and my beloved god-mother, Paralee Day, thank you for loving art and loving me. I am grateful for the Black tapestry of love and lore which my collective family has given me as a blueprint to build my own story.

To say I have a village to offer gratitude is an incredible understatement. I have an army. And that army is helmed by five-star generals who are beautiful inside and out. To "the Five" who set up a command center and managed everything from funeral arrangements and sleeping arrangements to court-day meal trains and later wedding plans, there are no words for what you have endured on my behalf and how we continue to support and honor each other every day. Tara Jones, Carmen Hughes, Wanda Witherspoon, Darnese Daniels, and Desreane Daniels, tragedy brought us closer together and there is not a mountain this sister circle can't climb.

From Grace Baptist Church to the Westchester Chapter of Jack and Jill of America, Inc. to my beloved "Ski Club," there are more people than I can possibly mention from different facets of my life. You sent a text without expecting a reply. You ran interference with onlookers who were more curious than concerned, you prayed for me and with me. You sent me heartfelt letters and still speak my daughter's name. I'm sure I'm not even aware of all your beautiful acts of sacrifice and generosity, but I have been lifted by them and I am incredibly grateful.

I MUST send a loving "shout-out" to my fellow Howard University alumni, particularly those with whom I performed as a drummer on the amazing H.U. "Thunder Machine" drumline and my illustrious sorority sisters of Alpha Kappa Alpha Sorority, Inc. I was one of fifty-three line sisters in spring 1990 at Alpha Chapter, and the beautiful "Diamonds" who stood with me all of those years ago are still standing with me today. You watched me become a woman. You stood with me during life's greatest highs and darkest lows. You sent me selfies wearing Gabrielle's button. You sat silently in affirmation during an ugly criminal trial. You took long day trips just to see my face. My life would not be as rich without my H.U. family.

God brings people into your life during every chapter, and I am incredibly grateful for my dear friends who I met in TV control rooms and corporate boardrooms. Coworkers turned friends who stood by me in the darkest hours. From Maureen White, who produced a tribute video of my baby that I hold close as a treasure, to Jessica Guff, Margo Baumgart, Phyllis McGrady, Derek Medina, Santina Leuci, Amy Entelis, Tory Johnson, Pat Langer, Helen Lynch, Lisa Goodnight, and so many more. You have shown up and stood up with me in so many ways, and I am forever grateful.

I have been lucky enough to walk among giants in my industry. Thank you to the many amazing people with equally amazing minds and hearts who have supported me and my work. To Robin Roberts, Gayle King, Diane Sawyer, Cheryl Richardson, Mellody Hobson, Barbara Corcoran, Shelley Ross, and Cara Stein . . . you each in your own special way cheered me on and encouraged me to always keep writing. Your partnership, mentorship, and love have meant the world.

Writing your first book, especially one so deeply personal, is a daunting proposition. However, there are people who have seemingly laid down the yellow bricks for me to follow throughout this journey and they collectively brought me to this moment. To George and Matthew Hiltzik, my long-time agent and my "brother from another mother," thanks for believing in me, pushing me, and challenging me to "bet on myself." To my rock star CAA literary agent, Cait Hoyt, I am so grateful that you saw a cardinal outside your window during our first conversation. Your faith in my heart and vision have made this all possible. To Leah Miller and Atria Books, thank you for taking a shot on me. Leah, your passion and care for Gabrielle's story, and my story, will never ever be forgotten. To Tracey Michae'l Lewis-Giggetts, my literary partner-in-crime, you took the endless stream-of-consciousness journal entries, notes, posts, and emails and placed the puzzle pieces in just the right way so I could see the gaps left to fill. Thank you for joining me on this journey and always fighting to honor my baby. To trauma therapist Caroline Kern, thank you for letting me "borrow your confidence" on this long and winding road to recovery. And to Rev. Dr. Franklin Richardson, thank you for being there from day one and affirming that I could use what was meant for evil and somehow offer it as a gift of inspiration.

Acknowledgments

If you have ever given me a blank notebook, responded to a journal entry I sent you in the middle of the night, asked me if I was still writing, or pushed me to keep moving on my writing journey, the completion of this project is because of your commitment to bring my words to life.

And while no one has ever accused me of knowing *anything* about cars, I now know exactly what an "axle" does. An axle conducts the power that turns the wheels and supports the car's weight. Every car needs an axle to move and operate. To *my* beloved Axel, thank you for listening to the little voice that told you to turn and look for me on the beach that day. You have somehow found a way to support the weight of my journey and have given me the fuel through your love to keep fighting as a hope warrior each and every day.

Finally, to the Gabrielle's Wings board of directors, my daughter's dear friends, classmates and their families, and all of you who financially support or volunteer with Gabrielle's Wings, thank you for saying my baby's name and giving wind to the wings that help children around the world dream new dreams and soar to new heights.

Yet will I trust Him.

About the Author

MICHELLE D. HORD is a creative storyteller and media executive. She is a graduate of Howard University and currently serves on the School of Communications' Board of Visitors. She is also a member of Alpha Kappa Alpha Sorority, Inc.

Michelle is the president of Hope Warrior, Inc., and former vice president of creative content and talent management at NBCUniversal. She has spent more than three decades in network news and entertainment. In a career that has spanned from television control rooms to corporate boardrooms, Michelle has consistently sought out opportunities to inspire creativity in all of its various forms. In 2018, she founded Gabrielle's Wings, Inc., a nonprofit organization dedicated to giving children of color in vulnerable communities the kind of experiences, access, and exposure that she is unable to now give her late daughter, Gabrielle Eileen.